PERSPECTIVES
of San Diego Bay

PERSPECTIVES
of San Diego Bay

A FIELD GUIDE

by the students of
THE GARY AND JERRI-ANN JACOBS
HIGH TECH HIGH

Foreword by Jane Goodall

Next Generation Press
Providence, Rhode Island

A High Tech High student production published by
Next Generation Press
P.O. Box 603252
Providence, RI 02906
www.nextgenerationpress.org

Printed in Hong Kong by South Sea International Press, Ltd.

Designed and edited by Chandler Garbell and Evan Morikawa

ISBN 0-9762706-5-X

10 9 8 7 6 5 4 3 2 1

Foreword
by Jane Goodall

Perspectives of San Diego Bay is a unique field guide—indeed, it is quite extraordinary. It was hand delivered to me by Jay Vavra in my seventeenth-floor hotel room overlooking San Diego Bay. I have known Jay for nine years, ever since he first got involved in Roots & Shoots, the Jane Goodall Institute's conservation and humanitarian education program for youth. And this field guide represents an end product of Jay's Roots & Shoots group at High Tech High school in San Diego. Jay, along with his teaching partners, Tom Fehrenbacher in the humanities and Rod Buenviaje in math, have mentored a very creative and versatile group of students to produce this wonderful book. Now I could look out of my windows and over the bay and, with book in hand, learn something of the history, geography, and biology of San Diego Bay, and also about the threats to the ecosystem as a whole.

One of the primary goals of Roots & Shoots is to help young people better understand the environment around them and to use this knowledge to take positive action to make the world a better place for all living things. *Perspectives* is a superb example of the kind of work that motivated and environmentally aware high school students can do when empowered to act. High Tech High has proved its ability to deliver a very high standard of environmental education, and the Roots & Shoots program requires that students pursue their interests outside the classroom. This particular group of HTH students, by integrating rigorous science with humanitarian principles, are learning to understand their community and their environment from a whole variety of perspectives. This has fostered in many of them a desire for action. The result of all this is that they have produced this incredibly well researched, informative and sensitive book. It will be useful for the people who live, work, and play in the Bay area—a place of great natural beauty that has been extensively developed, too often at the expense of its wildlife.

The students have seen for themselves the beauty and biodiversity of those areas of the Bay that have been protected, observed how easily we can damage such places, but noted too how effective conservation efforts can be. Not content with merely presenting their results clearly and concisely, they have become advocates for better environmental stewardship. They have taken the problems to heart and prescribed solutions to many of them, outlining a course of action that will help to revitalize the Bay and lead to a more healthy environment for both wildlife and humans. It is the kind of material that can impress lawmakers, for these young people of today are the voters and the leaders of tomorrow.

I was in San Diego to present the keynote address at the 25th Annual ESRI Users Conference for Geographic Information Systems. And I was excited to find that Jay and several of these students were presenting also, sharing with the audience some of the methods and technology that had informed sections of this book. They clearly demonstrated the importance of using GIS technology as a teaching tool in conservation biology: it had enabled them to have a much better understanding of complex, ecosystem level, biogeography. They attended the conference as representatives of Roots & Shoots, and I met with them and was so proud of them—and of Jay.

Most people will be amazed to think that high school students have produced this guide. I am no longer amazed by the capabilities of informed and empowered youth. There are Roots & Shoots groups in more than 90 countries, many of them involving high school students. Indeed, though it now provides materials for all ages, from pre-school through university and beyond, the program began with a group of high school students in Tanzania. It is immensely reassuring to know that the energy, enthusiasm and passions of youth can, under the mentorship of dedicated and wise adults like Jay, Rod, and Tom, lead to the production of a field guide like this. It gives me reason for hope. Hope for the future of our much abused planet. Hope that the youth of today will be better stewards than we have been and will gradually restore the health of our much abused planet.

Dr. Jane Goodall, DBE
Founder, Jane Goodall Institute
and U.N. Messenger of Peace
www.janegoodall.org

Introduction

One of our city's greatest natural and man-made resources is the San Diego Bay. To the visitor, the Bay's wildlife, shape and contour seems to have always existed just so. But the visitor is, in fact, presented with only the latest picture in a long series of changes in the San Diego Bay and its feathered, shelled, scaly, and fur-covered inhabitants. Once a mudflat delta opening of the San Diego River, at best 15 feet deep, the Bay now incorporates miles of harbor, boating and recreational facilities, military bases, constructed islands, downtown boardwalks, rock boulder–armored shoreline, and more.

As teachers of biology, mathematics, and humanities, we selected San Diego Bay to serve as the focus for our work for several reasons. First, we wished to provide our students with access and contact to a local natural environment. We did this to address increased insensitivity and detachment of so many urban dwellers — "nature deficit syndrome," in the words of Richard Louv. By providing our students greater contact with nature in this project, we hoped to give them an opportunity to critically examine and weigh the impact of human change upon the environment whose very health and well-being are essential to humanity. As teachers in a project-driven school, we hold that the production of meaningful and important student work is essential to learning. The project also empowers students and shows them the vital role and contributions they can make toward their community. The completion of this Field Guide project allowed our students to ask essential questions regarding the sustainability of our environment, the life of an urban ecology, and their place in such changing environments. As teachers, we hope our project encouraged good habits of mind, with students posing questions that looked for connections, sought evidence, weighed significance, and took into account the importance of perspective.

Both the perspectives of the casual visitor and the concerned scholar are addressed in this Field Guide. In addition, our students included the perspectives inspired by the very different locations we visited around the Bay. Using the latest Geographic Information Systems (GIS) analysis, our students provided layers of information regarding each location from the differing perspectives of our classrooms' disciplines. Our approach to study is as diverse at the Bay itself, with stories told by the marine life that live on its shores and by the boats that float across its surface. In short, we have attempted to create and provide a study in biogeography entitled.

Our students' biogeographical analysis, quantification and qualification of species, reflections, conclusions, conjectures and musings make up this Field Guide. Given the Bay's vastness, multiple uses, diverse ecology, and conflicting demands for its use and enjoyment, we asked our students to integrate many differing perspectives, attempting to destroy the artificial divisions between academic disciplines. Inspired by biology's regard for the study of life, our students used the tools of mathematics to quantify their work in mapping and in the graphical presentation of data, and the humanities provided a human framework that underlies everything through the principles of complexity, connection, and compassion.

We have been guided in our endeavors through the kind and continuing assistance of the scholars with San Diego GIS Educational Consortium, the insight and professionalism of the scientists at Scripps Institution of Oceanography and its Marine Physical Lab, the inspiration and environmental wisdom of Dr. Jane Goodall, and the clarity and predictive value of work on the natural history of civilizations by Professor Jared Diamond. Throughout its varied chapters, we hope, this Field Guide will provide the casual reader and policy maker alike with specific and detailed information, a vision of the area's environmental health, the importance of continued stewardship of this great natural resource, and words of caution and guidance for the future of the San Diego Bay. We hope this book represents more than a simple classroom lesson, and that the student research presented here provides important baseline measurements for future scientists and stewards of the Bay. May this guide provide future references and comparisons for related metropolitan bays, and for future changes along all our beautiful and fragile shores.

Jay Vavra, biology teacher
Tom Fehrenbacher, humanities teacher
Rodrigo Buenviaje, mathematics teacher
Grade 11, High Tech High
San Diego, California

Acknowledgments

The students of High Tech High extend their deepest gratitude for the support, advice, guidance, and efforts of Dr. Jay Vavra (biology), Mr. Tom Fehrenbacher (humanities) and Mr. Rodrigo Buenviaje (mathematics). Without them, this book would have been a mere shadow of what it is today.

Photos by Chandler Garbell, Zeke Koziol, Christina Hernandez, Jesse Lawrence, and Dr. Jay Vavra. Satellite and aerial photography is courtesy of the USGS and the IGPP Visualization Center.

We would like to thank the team member support of the Geographic Information Systems, a Scalable Skills Certification Program in GIS, a National Science Foundation-Advanced Technological Education Research Partnership between San Diego Mesa College, San Diego State University, and San Diego City Schools. Specials thanks go to Anthony Howser for his tireless efforts and for his mastery of mapping.

Thanks to the San Diego Historical Society, especially Cindy Krimmel, for helping organize our research. A special thank you to Muriel Strickland for her help on San Diego Bay mapping history. Mrs. Strickland provided unparalleled access to San Diego Historical Society's archives. She served as a close mentor and adviser in research of San Diego Bay maps. This could not have been done without her.

The identification and analysis of fauna in this guide was supported by several individuals in the scientific community. Thanks to Professor Paul Dayton of Scripps Institution of Oceanography for his critical review of our speculation on sea anemone abundance. Also thanks to Dr. Kirk Fitzhugh, Associate Curator of Polychaetes at the Los Angeles Natural History Museum for demystifying the mysterious segmented worms of the Bay.

Finally, thanks to James Jim Peugh of the San Diego Audubon Society, one of the most respected and influential environmental conservationists, for his assistance on the "Environmental Stewards of the Bay."

A warm acknowledgment to Jane Goodall for her inspiration to bring together knowledge, compassion and action in this book. As participating members of her educational program, Roots & Shoots, we strive to make a difference in our community and demonstrate that we can make a difference for all living things.

Thanks to the staff and ships' crews of the Nimitz Marine Facility for "showing us the ropes" and everything else involved in the oceanographic research of SIO. Also thanks to Wayne Nuzzolo of Midway Magic for coordination of our field trip to the Midway Museum.

Special gratitude for the Regional Occupational Program and What Kids Can Do for providing the financial support that allowed us to do our research on the Bay.

We appreciate the expertise of Professor William Newman of Scripps Institute of Oceanography, UCSD, in identifying the acorn barnacle Balanus amphitrite. We thank Emeritus Professor Russel Zimmer of USC for identifying the elusive Watersipora bryozoa from an image taken at the Boat Channel. Professor Gerald Bakus of USC assisted in narrowing in on the identification of the sponge Halichondria panacea. Finally, Daniel Gieger and James McLean of the Los Angeles Natural History Museum lent their expertise in identifying the mollusk Crepidula spinosum.

Finally, we thank Gary and Jerri-Ann Jacobs, Larry Rosenstock, and the faculty and staff of High Tech High, for their work to help keep project-based learning a reality. Without this approach to education our Field Guide would have never been possible.

Contents

Northern Pintail	Kevin Cisneros Alex Chee	54
Common Merganser	Maria Zimmerman	55
Redheaded Duck	Maria Zimmerman	55
Surf Scoter	Maria Zimmerman	56
PACIFIC FLYWAY	Ricky Gonzalez	**56**
AVES: SHOREBIRDS	Ross Zafar	**57**
Willet	John Horn	58
Marbled Godwit	Derrek Gudino Max Abbey	58
Western Gull	Kevin Strong	59
Great Blue Heron	Sabrana Boyd	59
Lesser Blue Heron	Stephen Csanadi Jeff Lathrop	60
Snowy Egret	Daniel Schultheis	60
Long-billed Curlew	Carly Pandza	61
Solitary Sandpiper	Eliot Ross	61
AVES: DIVING BIRDS	Alex Bethea Evan Morikawa	**62**
Belted Kingfisher	Christina Hernandez	63
Brandt Cormorant	Zach Barhoumi	63
Double-crested Cormorant	Jon Smith	64
Eared Grebe	Khoa Tran	64
Pied-bill Grebe	Tim Fox Tim Miller	65
Western Grebe	Ricky Gonzalez Eboni Hilliard	65
California Least Tern	Zeke Koziol Chandler Garbell	66
Brown Pelican	Tim Fox Patricia Atalla	66
Elegant Tern	Ben Lewis	67
Common Loon	Maria Zimmerman	67
AVES: RAPTORS	Nate Heiderer	**68**
Osprey	Nate Heiderer	69
Red-shouldered Hawk	Nate Heiderer	69
AVES: PERCHING BIRDS	Christina Hernandez	**70**

Intent of Study

The San Diego Bay Field Guide is a diverse exploration into the many facets of life, civilization, culture, and history of the Bay. By merging cartography, humanities, biology, and art, we created a comprehensive guide that not only explains concepts and creatures, but also draws connections between the possibilities that exist within the waters of San Diego.

These waters are not dead by any means. Even through enduring industrialization and development, marine creatures still thrive in certain areas throughout the Bay. Some of the most interesting and dissimilar creatures appear in the intertidal zones along the shoreline. As the tides are pulled away by the moon and the sun, vast expanses of life are uncovered. This guide provides insight into the many creatures that live and thrive in these areas between the tides. From the simplest sponge to the many sea birds and marine mammals, the San Diego Bay Field Guide offers quick ways to identify some of the common species found around the Bay during a scientific expedition or a casual stroll. If the original and highly detailed photographs and information are not enough to identify a creature, a dichotomous key has also been provided to identify an organism based on a series of questions and simple observations.

Not only does this book provide information on the various animals of the San Diego Bay, it also includes a scientific study on the distribution of the more common animals. One key aspect of the Bay is that no two areas are exactly the same. As the Bay gets used for various purposes, the life in different areas inevitably changes as well. In order to document, observe, and analyze these shifts, a biodiversity study was conducted at six locations around the Bay. Surveys, analysis, and observation were carried out from the Boat Channel by the old Naval Training Center, to the historic Spanish Landing near Harbor Island, to the tip of Shelter Island, to the Ferry Landing on Coronado Island, to America's Cup Harbor, and the Scripps Nimitz facility in Point Loma.

To add extra dimension to the study, advanced cartography and mapping systems were used to plot biodiversity results on high resolution satellite imagery of the Bay. Through collaboration with the University of San Diego, Geographic Information Systems (GIS) were used to plot biodiversity surveys using high accuracy Global Positioning Systems (GPS). Data was then overlaid onto the satellite image using a computer to create magnificent maps that gave spatial, not just quantitative, information about the organisms around the Bay.

To parallel the scientific aspects of these endeavors, this guide also embraces the beauty of thought, nature, and reflection in order to join the sciences and the arts in harmony. The many research expeditions made in order to create the major part of this book were paused for an hour or two to allow imaginations and inspiration from nature to soar. As a result, this guide is filled with poems and prose whose subjects stretch from simple musings on the beauty of the waterfront, to lengthy commentaries on the importance of ecological conservation. In the analysis of nature, history, and culture, the meanings of both humanity and human interactions were pondered upon and interpreted. When one looks around and sees drainage pipes, concrete blocks, and pollution to one side with one eye, and fish, mollusks, and sea lions with the other, the task to find the connection and the change between nature and civilization is an interesting one indeed.

It is this merging of thoughts and ideas that this guide hopes to embrace and explore in an attempt to bring the different perspectives of the San Diego Bay together in a comprehensive field guide for your perusal. We hope our studies inform and inspire you to explore the many different parts of the Bay and discover for yourself which perspective you like the best.

INTEGRATED PROJECT-BASED LEARNING

BIOLOGY
Animal Observation
Animal Photography
Species and Phyletic Writing
Dichotomous Keys
Food Web

Ecological survey techniques
Analysis of species distribution and abundance

Biogeography

Geographic Information Systems

Interaction of biology and place
Environmental Activism
Nature Reflections
Etymology of scientific names

MATH
Mapping Techniques
Geographic Information Systems Analysis

History of Mapping
Location Descriptions

HUMANITIES
Poetry
Place Descriptions
Location History
Description and Feelings
Stories

PERSPECTIVES

of San Diego Bay

The San Diego Bay is full of many marvelous and wonderful creatures from almost every phylum present in the Kingdom of Animalia. The ingenuity of nature and diversity of life were quite evident as we traveled from one location to the next, performing our research and sitting on the shores to do our nature reflections. Many of these creatures were found while collecting data from transects, whereas others were gleefully stumbled upon during an idle exploration of a site or simply by chance. These are the fauna of the Bay, the truly multidimensional representatives of the beauty of biology.

FAUNA
OF THE SAN DIEGO BAY

**Exploring Life in the
San Diego Bay**

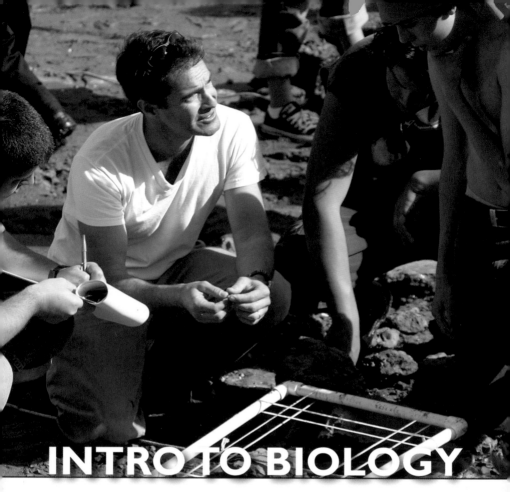

INTRO TO BIOLOGY

T
he intricacies of life have confounded, challenged, and puzzled scientists since the beginning of modern man. What is this mysterious aspect of the universe that we call life? The quest to understand this question and to grasp the reason behind all living things has become the impetus behind the study of biology. To study biology is not just to study that which is around us, but to study and define life itself. There can be no science without life, and as such there can be no life without science.

Throughout this guide, life is discussed and analyzed in all of its forms. Biology is the backbone of this book and connects all of the guide's many features. As we peer through crevices, under rocks, and in the sands of the intertidal zones, we become aware of life everywhere. In an attempt to make conclusions, we must first photograph, classify, and describe the natural history of the creatures in this guide. A brief guide of animals describes the attributes of many common intertidal creatures found throughout the Bay and categorizes them based upon phyla and evolutionary development. By progressing from the simplest sponge, through mollusks and up to vertebrate animals, the patterns and paths of evolution can be observed within the confines of San Diego Bay's intertidal zones.

In order to attain a complete understanding of biology, connections to the environment must be made. By studying not only the biodiversity of the San Diego Bay, but also its human aspects, history, and sociological connections, our scientific results can have a larger impact and meaning. It is this multitude of perspectives that causes the study of life to be enriching in avenues far beyond what most think of as just science.

The study of life is so diverse and complicated that it sometimes becomes hard to believe that such a phenomenon could have occurred naturally. Yet scientists and future scientists continue to study and experiment on life in order to gain a better understanding of the true nature of life; for if they can understand what life is and how it works, it may bring us closer to answering questions of human existence.

TAXONOMY

Taxonomy is the science of classification. All living things have been classified based upon their attributes and similarities. While some differences may be obvious, other differences between one species and another can be undetectably minute. Scientists have been attempting to classify living creatures since the time of Aristotle. Aristotle was able to classify living creatures by whether they fly, swim, or walk using only his culture's view of the world. Centuries later, as thousands of new creatures were discovered around the world, a man named Carolus Linnaeus published a means to classify new organisms and called it "Systema Naturae" in 1735. This system laid the foundations for modern scientific classification.

Modern classification organizes every living creature into multiple hierarchal categories. Here is an example of the classification of humans (*Homo sapiens*):

Kingdom: *Animalia*. The kingdom is the highest order of classification. There are 5 major kingdoms which include *animalia*, *plantae*, *monera* (bacteria), *fungi*, and *protista* (protozoans and algae).

Phylum: *Chordata*. The phylum is a large group of organisms that share similar evolutionary traits. Common animal phyla include chordatata (animals with backbones), mollusca (snails), arthropododa (insects), and echinodermata (sea urchins).

Class: *Mammalia*. The class is a grouping of organisms that share major physiological similarities. For example, all mammals are warm blooded, give live birth, and breathe air with lungs.

Order: *Primates*. The order is a smaller group of organisms that share a few physiological similarities. Primates include humans, apes, monkeys, and chimpanzees.

Family: *Hominidae*. The family represents closely related organisms separated by very few evolutionary and physiological differences. Others in the *Hominidae* family include extinct upright, bipedal primates such as Australopithecus, and *Homo erectus*.

Genus: *Homo*. The genus is the first part of the scientific name of any creature and represents morphologically similar organisms. Others in the homo genus include the extinct *Homo erectus*, and modern *Homo sapiens*.

Species: *H. sapiens*. The species is a group of related organisms that share a distinctive form and can produce viable offspring with each other. The *H. sapiens* are more commonly called humans.

When organisms are given scientific names, they are identified by genus, then species. For example, in *Homo sapiens*, the first word is the genus and the second is the species. This naming convention is constant throughout the scientific community. The naming of the genus and species is almost always in Latin, the language of science. The Latin words used to describe genus and species usually have translations related to the physiological aspects, appearance, or geographic location of an organism. The words *Homo sapiens* mean "knowing man," a tribute to the higher intelligence of the upright walking primates more commonly known as humans.

EVOLUTION

Where did life come from? Was it the chicken or was it the egg? Both of these questions have no definite answer and the best explanations are mere theories. However, the leading theory in the scientific community to explain the diversity and origins of life itself is called evolution. The principle, pioneered by Charles Darwin in the 1850s, has gained increasing amounts of evidence over the past 150 years and has worked out a plausible explanation to explain from the origins of life billions of years ago to modern humans.

The most common theory for the origins of life begins on an alien planet, or rather an alien looking planet earth. A mixture of toxic gasses such as carbon monoxide and carbon dioxide formed the violent atmosphere of primordial earth approximately 3.5 billion years ago. With a combination of meteors carrying water-ice, and the spark from lighting bolts, the essentials of oxygen, nitrogen, and carbon came together to form the first amino acids and hence started a billion year long chain reaction that led to the first forms of life.

The initial stages of life began as single celled-plants and bacteria. Trillions of algae turned the atmosphere into the breathable oxygen rich environment that we enjoy today. These single-celled creatures known as prokaryotes eventually merged with other simple prokaryotes and gave rise to the eukaryotic cell. The eukaryotic cell is one that has a nucleus and other organelles. This major division was a fundamental change that gave rise to all other multi-cellular organisms.

The eukaryotic cells began to combine and gave rise to simple multi-cellular organisms. The first multi-cellular organisms to appear on earth were the porifera, more commonly known as sponges. Even today, sponges remain the simplest multi-cellular organisms on the planet.

Animals continued to evolve and gave rise to cnidarians (jellyfish and sea anemones) and Platyhelminthes (flat worms). These creatures ruled the world around 500 million years ago. They introduced the concepts of specialized cells and the primordial beginnings of organs. Around 565 million years ago, an event known as the Cambrian explosion occurred and saw a massive increase in the diversity and number of creatures.

During this time, arthropods, round worms, and simple mollusks developed. Creatures began to gain exoskeletons, more developed organs and organ systems, and more complicated means of locomotion. Ancient seas were filled with trilobites (arthropods) and squid (mollusks). These major phyla are the most successful on the planet earth today and have the largest number of species, both above and below the water. Most animals on the planet are arthropods or mollusks.

As exoskeletons turned inward and began to calcify, the phyla chordata (animals with backbones) arose in the oceans. The first bony fish appeared nearly 450 million years ago. Around that time, plants and fungi appeared on land for the first time. Gills turned to lungs and fins turned to legs, giving rise to the first land animals.

Most of the animals found in the intertidal zones of the San Diego Bay are invertebrates and originate from creatures that developed very early in earth's evolutionary history. The vertebrates of the bay developed much later along the evolutionary ladder. Birds are the evolutionary remnants of ancient dinosaur raptors that developed lighter bones and grew feathers. As a meteor 65 million years ago killed off the larger dinosaurs, the ancestors of birds continued to evolve in their smaller forms to turn into what they are today.

Mammals began as the rodents of the dinosaur era. When the dinosaurs died off, less competition gave mammals an advantage which led to the rise of the mammals. Approximately 55 million years ago, the fish-loving mammals began to evolve to live closer and closer to their prey. As time went on, legs were lost to flippers and air holes went to the back of their necks. This was the beginning of many marine mammals such as dolphins and whales that are seen today. Eventually, primates took shape and evolved with increased cranial capacity and bipedal locomotion. For nearly 2 million years, modern *Homo sapiens* have developed into the civilization we are today.

Tips for Exploring the Intertidal Zones

1. Do not wear good shoes. Boots are best; otherwise use shoes that are expendable.

2. Beware of sink holes, as it is easy to lose shoes in them. They are often located near the shore and drainage pipes.

3. Organisms are often found under rocks and in small pools. Crabs, worms, octopi, and some kinds of fish can be found under rocks. Small fish are often found in pools when high tide becomes low tide. Shrimp and worms can also be found simply by digging in the mud.

4. Look for any movement on the ground. Many organisms are camouflaged and the only way to see them is to look closely for movement as you slowly move along the beach.

5. Bring a bucket to keep organisms in if you plan to take any for use as specimens.

6. Small fish in enclosed pools can usually be caught and kept as specimens easily because they are confined to the pool and cannot get away. One easy way to catch these fish is to dig a narrow channel from the pool down to the water and place a hand in the channel so that the water flows through the fingers, but the fish get caught in the hand. In pools that have many fish, one can simply cup both hands together, place them at the bottom of the pool, and pull the hands up. The hands act like a cup to hold both the fish and water, which slowly drains from the hands while the fish are placed in a bucket.

7. Always place rocks back in their original location when they are moved.

Wash hands after exploring in polluted bay waters!

Introduction to the Dichotomous Key

A man is walking down the beach at low tide and sees a fascinating creature. He wants to know what it is, but does not have a background in zoology. Luckily, he has access to the following dichotomous key to help him in his identification quest. A dichotomous key is merely a written tool to classify an object using a series of linking questions. The many connected questions will lead any reader to the identity of the unknown object through simple observation.

For example, pretend that you are staring at three different pieces of sport equipment. All you need to do is to answer the questions, then follow the directions and you will be able to identify the ball you are looking at.

1. Is the ball round?
   a. No – The ball is a football.
   b. Yes – Go to question 2.
2. Is the ball orange?
   a. No – The ball is a baseball.
   b. Yes – The ball is a basketball.

This simplistic example hopefully gives you a general idea of how to use the dichotomous key. If you carefully examine the creature that you are looking at, and answer the questions then follow the directions, this key should lead you to the animal that you are looking at. Just remember, BE PATIENT. This key may take a while to get though due to the complicated nature of life.

There are two different keys in this book. One is for all vertebrate animals (animals that have a backbone) and one for invertebrates (animals that do not have backbones). Be sure that you are using the proper key in your quest of identification.

DICHOTOMOUS KEY
VERTEBRATES

1. Does it have feathers?
a. Yes: Go to 12.
b. No: Go to 2.

2. Is it primarily found on water?
a. Yes: Go to 3.
b. No: Go to 10.

3. Does it have scales?
a. Yes: Go to 4.
b. No: Go to 9.

4. Does it have silver scales?
a. Yes: It is a silver smelt fish.
b. No: Go to 5.

5. Does it have mottled brown/black spots that form bars on its flanks?
a. Yes: It is a spotted sea bass.
b. No: Go to 6.

6. Does the body become larger, circular at the head?
a. Yes: It is a northern clingfish.
b. No: Go to 7.

7. Does it look like a small, gray/bluish whale with a pointy snout?
a. Yes: It is a dolphin.
b. No: Go to 8.

8. Is it greenish/reddish on its topside and bluish/tinted underneath?
a. Yes: It is a tidepool sculpin.
b. No: Go to 9.

9. Is it fairly large, furry brown and blubbery?
a. Yes: It is a sea lion.
b. No: Go to 1.

10. Is it covered more than 1/2 with fur or hair?
a. Yes: Go to 11.
b. No: It is a human.

11. Does it have 3 or 4 toes?
a. 3: It is a squirrel.
b. 4: It is a dog.

12. Is it a small bird, less than 10 inches long?
a. Yes: Go to 13.
b. No: Go to 17.

13. Does it have a red breast, forehead, and stripe over the eye and back?
a. Yes: It is a house finch.
b. No: Go to 14.

14. Does it have a long black bill?
a. Yes: It is a hummingbird.
b. No: Go to 15.

15. Does it have a brown belt-like stripe over its chest with a black crest?
a. Yes: It is a belted kingfisher.
b. No: Go to 16.

16. Is it roughly 5 inches with a large triangular head?
a. Yes: It is a black phoebe.
b. No: Go to 12.

17. Does it have long legs?
a. Yes: Go to 18.
b. No: Go to 23.

18. Is the color on the wing lining light brown cinnamon with a cinnamon buff belly?
a. Yes: It is a marbled godwit.
b. No: Go to 19.

19. Is the beak (long) orange and black towards the tip?
a. Yes: It is a willet.
b. No: Go to 20.

20. Is the plumage bluish gray?
a. Yes: It is a great blue heron.
b. No: Go to 21.

21. Is the plumage completely white (black beak)?
a. Yes: It is a snowy egret.

b. No: Go to 22.

22. Is there a crest off its head?
a. Yes: It is a lesser blue heron.
b. No: Go to 12.

23. Is it small and plump with gray plumage, red beady eyes?
a. Yes: It is a rock dove.
b. No: Go to 24.

24. Is the beak bright yellow with a red spot?
a. Yes: It is a western gull.
b. No: Go to 25.

25. Does it have webbed feet?
a. Yes: Go to 26.
b. No: Go to 31.

26. What color beak/bill does it have?
a. White bill: It is the American coot.
b. Multicolored bill with white, red, yellow and black, mainly orange and swollen at the base: It is the Surf Scooter.
c. Blue and black tipped bill with white crown: It is the redhead.
d. Bright yellow and blue beak: It is the double-crested cormorant.
e. Black pointed beak: It is a common loon.
f. Blue bill with small black nail at tip: It is a greater scaup.
g. Other: Go to 27.

27. Does it have two-tone purple and dark green plumage on the neck and head with a large white patch?
a. Yes: It is the bufflehead duck.
b. No: Go to 28.

28. Does it have a black head and upper neck, white breasts, flanks and belly?
a. Yes: It is the merganser duck.
b. No: Go to 29.

29. Does it have green plumage on the head and neck?
a. Yes: It is the mallard duck.
b. No: Go to 25.

30. Does it have tail feathers that come to a point?
a. Yes: It is the northern pintail duck.
b. No: Go to 25.

31. Does it have a long slender orange bill, and black legs?
a. Yes: It is the elegant tern.
b. No: Go to 31.

32. Does it have a forked tail and wings that come to a point with a blue head?
a. Yes: It is the barn swallow.
b. No: Go to 32.

33. Does it have a pointed bill, short legs and a forked tail?
a. Yes: It is the California least tern.
b. No: Go to 1.

DICHOTOMOUS KEY
INVERTEBRATES

I. Does it have an exoskeleton?
a. Yes – go to II.
b. No - go to III.

II. Does it have a segmented body?
a. Yes – arthropoda – go to VII.
b. No – mollusk – go to X.

III. Does it have 5-point symmetry?
a. Yes - giant sea star.
b. No – go to IV.

IV. Is it radially symmetric?
a. Yes – go to V.
b. No – breadcrumb sponge.

V. Is it flat?
a. Yes – encrusting bryozoan.
b. No – go to VI.

VI. Does it move?
a. Yes – cnidaria – go to XXII.
b. No – tunicate.

VII. It is attached to a rock?
a. Yes – striped barnacle.
b. No – go to VIII.

VIII. Does it have a forked tail and antennae?
a. Yes – rock louse.
b. No – go to IX.

IX. Does it have a soft shell?
a. Yes – red ghost shrimp.
b. No – striped shore crab.

X. Does it have eight appendages?
a. Yes – two-spotted octopus.
b. No – go to XI.

XI. Does it have a girdle?
a. Yes – mossy chiton.
b. No – go to XII.

XII. Does it have two tentacle-like antennae on one side?
a. Yes – go to XIII.
b. No – go to XV.

XIII. Is it yellowish in color?
a. Yes – dorid nudibranch.
b. No – go to XIV.

XIV. Is it bluish in color?
a. Yes – navanax.
b. No – California sea hare.

XV. Is it long, thin, and wavy?
a. Yes – scaled worm shell.
b. No – go to XVI.

XVI. Does it have a spiral shell?
a. Yes – go to XVII.
b. No – go to XVIII.

XVII. Is it bluish in color?
a. Yes – grey periwinkle.
b. No – slipper snail.

XVIII. Is it bluish-black?
a. Yes – bay mussel.
b. No – go to XIX.

XIX. Is it bi-valve?
a. Yes – Pacific oyster.
b. No – go to XX.

XX. Is it only partially covered by its shell?
a. Yes – bubble snail.
b. No – go to XXI.

XXI. Does it have deep ridges?
a. Yes – rough limpet.
b. No – file limpet.

XXII. Is it attached to a rock?
a. Yes – aggregated anenome.
b. No – burrowing anenome.

PORIFERA

PORIFERA

Sponges are the simplest of all the multicellular animals on our planet. They are marine, water-dwelling filter feeders that use a system of bodily canals and chambers opening outwards by way of pores to siphon water and food in and out of their bodies. Sponges lack organs, nervous systems, and muscles and are often mistaken for plants in their simplicity. There are approximately 5000 modern species of sponges known today, and each have been classified into one of three groups.

There are three main classes of the sponges: *Calcarea* (the calcareous sponges), *Hexactinellida* (the glass sponges), and *Demospongia* (the most common sponge). Members of the *Calcarean* class are sponges composed entirely of spicules, or fibers, made of calcium carbonate. They are most prolific in tropical, shallow waters, though a few species have been found in depths of 4000 feet. The next class of sponges, *Hexactinellida,* is considered to be one of the earliest branches within the *Porifera* because it contains sponges composed of extensive regions of syncitia, or multinucleate cytoplasm. As such, these sponges are very different than most others. *Hexactinellids* have siliceous spicules arranged in a formation similar to that of a toy jack, six rays intersecting at right angles, and can't contract in the way that other classes of sponges can.

The sponge, *Halichondria panacea,* most commonly seen around the lower intertidal zones of the San Diego Bay is classified as a member of *Demospongia*. This diverse class of sponge contains organisms made up of spongin fibers and/or siliceous spicules. Demosponges are often quite large and come in a variety of different forms. Some species inhabit the undersides of large rocks, encrusting surfaces with their entire bodies, whereas others form towering columns that almost mimic the structure of coral. They take on a variety of forms, from encrusting sheets living beneath stones to branching stalks towering upright.

BREADCRUMB SPONGE
Halichondria panacea

Class: *Demospongiae* | **Order:** *Halichondrida* |
Family: *Halichondriidae*
Morphology: Polymorphic. Varies from thin sheets to branched forms. Color varies; green in areas of light, otherwise yellow or orange.
Range: From Alaska to Baja.
Feeding: Filter feeders; capture food particles that are suspended in the water column.
Reproduction: Reproduction performed both asexual and sexual. Sperm and eggs are often released by the same individual and can occur at different times to avoid self-fertilization. Sperm is released by the sponge and carried by the water current towards another sponge. The fertilized egg gives rise to a flagellated larva, which swims freely and then attaches to the substrate.
Etymology: *Halichondria panacea* (S. *Hali* holy L. *chondros* cartilage Gk. *panicea* something that cures)
Other: Prevalent in Britain and Ireland. Found in damp habitats on the shore including rock pools, under boulders and overhangs. Underwater, it is particularly abundant in wave exposed or tide swept situations, often dominating kelp stipes. In low or variable salinity, it is likely to colonize foliose red algae.

CNIDARIA

CNIDARIA

The phylum *Cnidaria* contains some of the most beautiful - and some of the most dangerous - aquatic creatures in the ocean. If you've ever witnessed the awesome presence of a Portuguese man-o-war, whose opalescent tentacles deliver a painful injury to all that cross its path, you'll understand what we mean. All members of the Cnidarian phylum come equipped with stinging cells called nematocysts; just one casual touch to any Cnidarian organism will explain why Cnidarians are commonly referred to as "the stingers." Cnidarians are also characterized by a hydrostatic skeleton, meaning their entire bodies are little more than sacks of cells and water and that their movement is very fluid. This phylum is home to the sea anemone, coral, jellyfish, and sea pen, and contains over 15,000 different species spread throughout the world's oceans. Although they are the second-most simplistic marine creatures in the Animal Kingdom, Cnidarians are much more complex than the sponges of the phylum *Porifera* and are therefore challenging to explain.

Cnidarians are divided into two bodily forms: the medusoid form, which is most commonly seen in jellyfish and some forms of hydroids, and the polyp form, which is usually attributed to most species of sea anemone and coral. Medusa-type Cnidarians pulse and glide through the water without any idea where they're going due to a characteristic lack of a brain and basic nervous system. Polyps, on the other hand, are sessile and usually attach themselves to a strong surface. While most Cnidarians stick to one form or the other over the course of their lifetimes, some alternate between the stages and spend parts of their lives as a structurally different organism.

The main classes in the Cnidarian phylum are *Anthozoa, Hydrozoa, Scyphozoa,* and *Conulata*. The Anthozoa class contains creatures more commonly known as the "flower" Cnidarians; this would include sea anemones, true corals, and sea pens. *Anthozoans* are usually found in large colonies, though some species can be seen existing solitarily. The next class of *Cnidarians* is *Hydrozoa*. These Cnidarians include fire corals and other similar animals, like hydroids. Like Anthozoans, Hydrozoans are colonial, but while Anthozoans are mostly found as polyps, Hydrozoans can be either of the two Cnidarian forms. The third class of the phylum is the Scyphozoa, which contains all true jellyfish. Scyphozoa contains a sub-class known as Cubozoa; these jellyfish are actually box-shaped. Members of this class range in size from little more than twelve millimeters to an astonishing two meters across with tentacles reaching almost forty meters down! The last class of the Cnidarians is the Conulata; these cone-shaped Cnidarians became extinct during the Triassic period.

In San Diego Bay, the phyla Cnidaria is represented by the burrowing anemone and the aggregating anemone, which are found on the shores of Coronado.

BURROWING ANEMONE
Anthopleura artemisia

Class *Anthozoa* | **Subclass** *Zoantharia* | **Order** *Actiniaria* | **Family** *Actiniidae*
Morphology: The burrowing anemone has a body that is
around two inches in diameter, with a color of grey, brown,
or olive green. The anemone has tentacles that are pink,
orange, green or blue in color with bands of white.
Range: The burrowing anemone is found in the intertidal
zone from Alaska to Southern California.
Feeding: The burrowing anemone has small stinging
harpoon-like cells that can be aimed at passing by plankton,
small animals, and fish. These cells will paralyze the creature for the anemone to eat. Mussels and other sea animals
are sometimes washed into the reach of the anemone's
reach.

Locomotion: The giant sea anemone can move, slowly, using its suction cups, but the
anemone will mostly dig itself in the sand and stay there.
Reproduction: The burrowing anemone can reproduce sexually and asexually.
Etymology: *Anthopleura artemisia* (L. *Anthopleura* Stinging Flower; *artemisia* Gk.
Wormwood.)
Other: Nudibranchs feast on the tentacles of anemones. This makes the nudibranch
change color to give off a bright color which scares the nudibranchs predators. For its de-
fense, the anemone has a toxin that will paralyze sea creatures, but will not hurt humans.

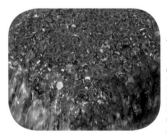

AGGREGATING ANEMONE
Anthopleura elegantissima

Class *Anthozoa* | **Order** *Actiniatia* | **Family** *Actiniidae*
Morphology: The aggregating anemone is a very
interesting looking organism. It can be around 2-5 cm
in diameter and grow to be around 4-5cm in height. The
crown around the top of the anemone expands the diameter to eight centimeters. The column is a light green
and white. The anemone can become a green olive color depending on what kind of algae
begins to live on it. It is much smaller then the burrowing anemone and can be commonly
found in large colonies.
Range: Mostly found on rocky shores, all along the western sea board. From Alaska all
the way down to the cost of Baja California. They can be found along rocks and sand
patches in bays.
Feeding: It is a carnivore; feeds on crustaceans
that pass by.
Locomotion: The *Anthopleura elegantissima*
does not relocate itself.
Reproduction: Reproduces both sexually and
asexually. Eggs are released in July but do not
appear until February. The colony that they live
in has its own special order for reproduction.
The outermost of the colony don't really reproduce. The inner of the colony are the ones who
reproduce. Most of the newborn are clones of the
inner colony that just keep on reproducing.
Etymology: *Anthopleura elegantissima* (L.
Anthopleura Stinging Flower; L. *elegantissima*
elegant)

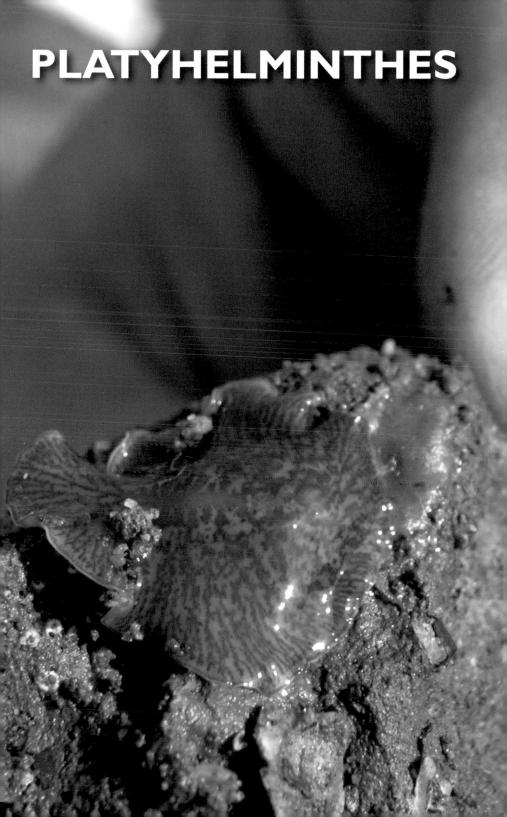

PLATYHELMINTHES

PLATYHELMINTHES

Members of the phylum *Platyhelminthes* are very aptly named; this group of flatworms contains over 20,000 different species of mostly parasitic worms that often look like small, wrinkly plastic pancakes. They are bilateral creatures, which means that if you were to slice a flatworm down its axis the resulting sides would be perfectly symmetrical. Flatworms come in many vibrant colors and patterns and can be found in both fresh and salt water. They can be anywhere from 0.4 mm to 25 meters long. The most well-known *Platyhelminthe* is the tapeworm.

Flatworms are slightly more advanced evolutionarily than the sponge or Cnidarian. They do not have a skeleton and instead possess a system of epidermal cilia that enables them to move from one place to the next. They have a very simple nervous system and two very basic brains, called ganglia, which are little more than two small bundles of nerves. Flatworms don't have eyes, but they do have eyespots that can vaguely sense light. They do not possess any formal respiratory system and instead absorb oxygen through their skin. Flatworms have a combined digestive/excretory system that processes food in and out of a flatworm's body through a single opening. Like a slug or snail, flatworms also possess a mucous gland that allows them to secrete a slime track that helps to glide over a surface using their epidermal cilia.

The main group of flatworms contains worms that are carnivorous parasites and/or scavengers. Some, like the tapeworm, are entirely parasitical, and live, reproduce, and die in the intestines of different animals. Some smaller and more unique species ingest micro algae, and become living greenhouses. They push the algae to outermost layers of their skin and then utilize the energy released by the photosynthesis of the algae. Most flatworms, however, are carnivorous and depend on a host to survive.

Flatworms are hermaphroditic; they have both male and female reproductive organs. Once two adult flat worms meet, they perform an odd 'dance' in which they move toward each other, touch, then roll around together while thrusting their penis papillae and stylets outward at each other. This event often causes damage to one or both of the partners but the wounds will heal within 24 hours. After one of the worms has successfully penetrated the other, it will hold on for several minutes, in which time it will inject sperm into the other worm. Flatworms can also reproduce by simply splitting in half.

Around the area of San Diego Bay, flatworms can commonly be found under rocks or at the lowest zone of a tide pool. If a flatworm wanders too close to the shoreline it will dry out and die. This is why they inhabit the lowest part of the tide pools.

BRYOZOA

Bryozoans are a prolific but mysterious set of marine creatures. Commonly known as "moss animals," the members of the *Bryozoa* phylum are colonial and are sometimes mistaken for corals, hydroids, or even some types of seaweed because their skeletons often grow in shapes and patterns similar to that of non-Bryozoans. Some encrust whatever substrate they're inhabiting, whereas others form lacy colonies that spread over many feet. The 5000 different species of the Bryozoan phylum often pose a nuisance to sailors, workmen and engineers because their colonies can grow so huge that they clog pipes and reduce ship maneuverability if they've taken up residence on the underside of a ship's hull. Members of this phylum possess hydrostatic skeletons.

Bryozoans are classified into three different groups: *Phylactolaemata, Stenolaemata,* and *Gymnolaemata.* The first classification, *Phylactolaemata,* contains fresh water Bryozoans. These organisms do not possess complex sensory organs like other Bryozoans. The second classification, *Stenolaemata,* contains marine Bryozoans. *Stenolaemata* breaks into five different sub-groups based on colony structure: *Trepostomata* contains Bryozoans that group together in massive, hearty colonies; *Cystoporta* and *Cryptostomata* contain organisms that colonize together in very delicate networks; organisms in *Fenestrata* make net-like structures; and *Tubuliporata* contains Bryozoans that colonize in tubes. After *Stenolaemata* and its sub-groups, Bryozoans can be classified as members of *Gymnolaemata,* a marine class of organisms that are very flat. This class is divided into two sub-groups: *Cenotomata* and *Cheilostomata,* which divide Bryozoans into uncalcified and calcified structures, respectively.

An interesting fact about Bryozoan colonies is that they are organized a lot like a city. Different individuals within each colony assume different roles and carry out special functions that benefit the whole of each colonial unit: some gather food, others are devoted to protecting and strengthening the colony, where others perform colony maintenence to keep their home clean.

ENCRUSTING BRYOZOAN   *Watersipora sp.*

Class: *Gymnolaemata* | **Order**: *Cheilostomata* | **Family**: *Watersiporidae*
Morphology: Microscopic sea animals which live in colonial structures. They form colonies that appear as thin porous sheets on hard surfaces and are formed like fossils. They also have many different forms as well, such as finger-shaped, fan-shaped, mats, and spiraling fans. They measure an average of 0.8 x 0.4 mm in size. Averages of twenty-one individual *Watersipora* are present in a colony.
Locomotion: Sessile
Range: Inhabits warm waters such as the Gulf of Mexico; range from Florida to Brazil including Southern California, the Gulf of Mexico and the Caribbean.
Feedinf: Bryozoans feed off microscopic organisms that float in the water. They eat these organisms by latching onto them with their tentacles.
Reproduction: Asexually, Watersipora reproduce from November to April with the peak in November and December.
Other: Most abundant in the winter months and tolerant of a wide range of temperatures.

ECHINODERMATA

T he major classes of *Echinodermata* include *Crinoidea, Echinoidea, Asteroidea, Ophiurodiea,* and *Holithuriudea.* Many *Crinoidea* are common known as sea lilies. Echinoidea is the class for sea urchins. Asteroidea includes all starfish. *Ophiurodiea* is brittle stars. The final class *Holithuriudea* is made up of sea cucumbers.

The most basic and well-known fact about echinoderms structure is their five-part radial symmetry. The skeletal system of echinoderms is unique as is their water vascular system. Their skeletons are made of interlocking calcium carbonate plates and spines. These plates are in all echinoderms, but vary in size and spacing. In a sea urchin, for example, the plates are much smaller and closer together than those in a sea star. These plates are not solid blocks; electron microscopes reveal that these are actually fine networks of calcium carbonate structures known as stereom. Several internal structures, like the tube feet of the water vascular system for example, protrude through the gaps in the skeleton. Another interesting part of the morphology of echinoderms is pedicellaria, which are small skeletal structures used to keep small organisms from settling on their body. Coelom, a large fluid-filled cavity lined by tissue, large gonads and a complete gut are also part of echinoderms. Many echinoderms also have the unique ability to turn their stomach out their mouth in order to digest food outside the body. The water vascular system takes over the circulatory and respiratory system in echinoderms, as they lack those systems.

The nervous system of echinoderms is primitive. There is no central brain, merely ganglia that control the body. This gives echinoderms interesting behavior. Any part of an echinoderm can react to the environment it encounters.

The water vascular system is something of a hydraulics system. This system uses water pressure through axial tubes of the body to move, grab and eat. The system consists of 3 main parts: the axial tubes stretching through the body, the ampulla and the podia (tube feet). The ampulla contracts and expands to move the tube feet up and down for suction. The suction is used to control the pressure to create locomotion and capture food.

In the survey, only one echinoderm was found; that was *Pisaster giganteus*, a giant sea star. Though echinoderms are the largest pure sea water phylum, we could only find that one sea star. One reason for this might be that most echinoderms do not venture into the intertidal zone, preferring being submerged in water all the time. Sea lilies and brittle stars are never seen above water, as they cannot survive. Though sea urchins and sea stars can be in the intertidal zone, they prefer the lower submerged areas.

GIANT SEA STAR
Pisaster giganteus

Class *Asteroidia* | **Order** *Forcipulatida* | **Family** *Asterinidae*

Morphology: Recognizable by a ring of blue basal integument surrounding its spines. Ring is surrounded by ring of brown pedicellariae. Pedicellariae are plier shaped and function as deterrents against other organisms. Spines are white-tipped on the adults and blue-violet or pink on juveniles. Arm's radius is over 30 cm.

Range: Can be found all along the California coast as well as the Mexican coast. Often seen in low sub tidal regions in protected areas, ranging from the intertidal zone to 88 meters depth. Can also be found on sand rocks and pier pilings.

Feeding: Feeds upon snails, Chitons and barnacles. In studies in Santa Barbara, a sea star chose from several food items in the following order:

1. Mussel *Mytilus edulis* and *M. californianus*
2. Ribbed mussel *Septifer bifurcates*
3. Snail *Nucella emarginata*
4. Snails *Acanthina spirata* and *Tegula funebralis*
5. Chiton *Nuttallina californica*.

Locomotion: Locomotion powered by water vascular system.

Reproduction: Free spawners-spawning occurs in March or April of each year.

Etymology: *Pisaster* giganteus (*L. Pisaster*, multiple fish star; *L. giganteus*, gigantic

Other: Found near mussel beds in San Diego Bay, but rare since it has been collected as a curio for years.

MOLLUSCA

MOLLUSCA

Mollusca (L. *mollis* meaning soft) is one of the three most successful groups in the animal kingdom. Over 160,000 species have been described, of which around 128,000 are living and about 35,000 are recorded as fossil species. Mollusks are found in nearly all habitats. In the sea they inhabit regions from the deepest ocean trenches to the intertidal zone. They may be found in freshwater as well as on land where they occupy a wide range of habitats. The phylum Mollusca contains eight classes: *Gastropoda, Pelecypoda, Cephalopoda, Aplacophora, Monoplacophora, Polyplacophora, Scaphopoda,* and *Caudofoveata.* The most advanced class of living mollusks is the *Gastropoda,* which comprises more than 80% of all living mollusk species.

The *Gastropoda* have approximately 40,000 living species. Most gastropods have shells; however, there are quite a few groups that have either reduced or internal shells, or no shell at all. Shelled forms are generally called "snails" and forms without shells are called "slugs"; however, terrestrial slugs are not closely related to the various marine slugs as one might think. Although most gastropods are marine, there are numerous forms in both freshwater and terrestrial environments. The San Diego Bay houses many kinds of gastropods. The snails found in the bay include file limpets, rough limpets, gray periwinkles, slipper snails, and the tube snails. The other kinds of gastropods found in the bay are slugs. We found bubble snails, many navanax, a dorid nudibranch, and a sea hare.

The *Pelecypoda* includes the bivalves, which are laterally compressed animals, with two shell "valves" that are hinged on the animal's dorsal surface. They are found in just about every marine environment, from the intertidal zone to the deepest marine habitats. They are suspension feeders, filtering small organisms and organic particles from the water such as bacteria, phytoplankton, zooplankton, and nonliving organic detritus. Only two kinds of creatures have been found in the San Diego Bay. They are the bay mussels and Pacific oysters.

The *Cephalopoda* include the familiar squid and octopus. They are the most intelligent and the fastest swimming aquatic invertebrates. This family includes squid, octopi, and cuttlefish. Cephalopods have a closed circulatory system, which is an adaptation to their active lifestyle, as opposed to the open circulatory system found in other Mollusks. There has been only one *Cephalopoda* found in the San Diego Bay: the two-spot octopus.

The *Polyplacophora* are commonly known as chitons. These mollusks have seven or eight dorsal shell plates, although they may be covered mostly or entirely by soft tissue in some species. The approximately 600 described species are generally flattened and elongated animals that are typically found in the intertidal zone grazing on epibenthic algae. The chiton commonly found in the San Diego Bay is the mossy chiton.

FILE LIMPET
Lottia limatula

Class *Gastropoda* | **Order** *Archaeogastropoda* | **Family** *Acmaeidae*
Morphology: Made of a fleshy mantle that secretes
calcareous shell. Bilaterally symmetric (if cut in half, both
halves would be similar). The shell is conical with fine
beading on the surface that radiates out from the apex.
Range: Enjoys staying in the cold waters of Atlantic and
Pacific Ocean.
Feeding: Herbivores, or plant eaters, during the day. Eat
marine vegetation and marine algae. Able to do this using
their radula, a tongue-like organ with thousands of tiny
denticles.
Locomotion: Moves around during the day by rippling
its muscle of the foot in a wave-like form. Returns every night to the same exact place it
resides. Nobody knows why or how they do this.
Reproduction: Have separate sexes. Reproduction occurs in the winter. Spawning of
olive-green eggs occurs in January, February, April and October.
Etymology: *unknown*
Other: Has a head with a mouth. Has two long tentacles with a black eye at each end.

ROUGH LIMPET   *Lottia scabra*

Class *Gastropoda* | **Order** *Archaeogastrocpoda* | **Family** *Acmaeidae*
Morphology: Characterized by a rough oval shell in the shape of a
cone. One fourth the width, the shell has ribs and a scalloped margin.
Shell is greenish brown. Rough Limpets, in comparison to File Lim-
pets, have larger ridges that stand out about one mm.
Range: Oregon to southern Baja.
Feeding: Eat diatoms from rocks using iron-based teeth. Leave dents in the rocks where
they feed for the micro-plants.
Locomotion: Move using a foot muscle under the shell. Usually move when in search for
more food. Can stay on the same rock for over twenty years.
Reproduction: Lay eggs. Have different genders but no interest in mating. Use a mechanism called broadcast spawning. Broadcast spawning is the mechanism in which males
and females release large amounts of gametes into the ocean. These gametes mix and
create offspring.
Etymology: *Lottia scabra* (L. *Lottia* unknown, L. *scabra* Rough surface, scabs).

BUBBLE SNAIL   *Bulla Gouldiana*

Class *Gastropoda* | **Subclass** *Orthogastropoda* | **Order** *Cephalaspide* | **Suborder** *Bullacea*
Family *Bullidae*
Morphology: Shells are mostly brownish or yellowish, round or ridged.
Range: The Bubble Snail is found living on rocks from California to Ecuador.
Feeding: Tend to feed on algae. They eat particles of brush
and scrape from the surfaces of rocks and seaweed.
Locomotion: Inch their way along the ocean floor using their
two pairs of feelers to find their way. Gastropods crawl using
a large, muscular foot. The muscles in the foot wave in a rippling motion that causes the snail to move forward.
Reproduction: Bubble Snails court from 15 minutes to six
hours before they have sex, touching with tentacles, as well
as biting on the lip and genitals. Bubbles Snails reproduce by
releasing embryo masses. They lay yellow jelly-like eggs on
seaweed growing on the mud, sea lettuce, or sea spaghetti.
Some reproduce asexually.
Etymology: *Bulla gouldiana* (L. *Bulla* Bubble; L. *gouldiana* Gould's).

SLIPPER SNAIL
Crucibulum spinosum
Class: *Mollusca* | **Order**: *Neotaenioglossa* | **Family**: *Calyptraeidae*
Morphology: Distinct tan-colored shell with small reddish-brown spots on its surface, and a straight or only slightly convex edge on the internal shelf; 3 to 5 cm across; the underside of the shell has a shelf-like deck which forms a niche for the animal to withdraw into. All slipper snails are born male. When they're two months old, they start changing into females. After several weeks, the change is complete—the males have become females.
Range: Southern California; typically found attached to shells and stones on soft substrate around the low water mark.
Feeding: The slipper snail feeds by filtering water through its gills, which are covered with mucous. It moves the food particles to its mouth by way of its cilia.
Locomotion: Adult slipper snails lead a sedentary life, stacking themselves on the shells of other snails, with smaller ones sitting atop larger ones.
Reproduction: To reproduce, male slipper snails deposit sperm under a female's shell. Her eggs hatch into larvae that stay put until they've developed into exact miniatures of adult snails. Periodically, females lift their shells and, with their heads, push the juveniles out into the cold marine world. Newly hatched young can't cling well, so they sink to the bottom, where they scrape algae from rocks. Eventually they're able to cling to host snails, like their parents, where most become immobile—even depending on the host snail to carry them away from predators.
Etymology: *Crecibulum spinosum* (L. *crecibulum* earthen pot, L. *spinosum* thorny).

GRAY PERIWINKLE
Littorina planaxis
Class *Gastropoda* | **Subclass** *Prosobranchia* | **Order** *Mesogastropoda* | **Family** *Littorinidae* | **Subfamily** *Littorininae*

Morphology: 1/2—3/4" (13—19 mm) high, almost as wide. Broadly oval-shaped, narrow body. Brownish-gray, with irregular, scattered whitish spots. Aperture is dark brown, with a white spiral band at bottom.
Range & Habitat: Charleston, Oregon, USA to Bahia Magdalena, Baja California, Mexico. Found on rocks along shoreline above high tide line. Spend most of life out of the water. Occupy highest vertical position on shore of all marine molluscan species in California.
Feeding: Microscopic algae and diatoms, but radula also scrapes pieces off larger seaweeds. Feeds by "licking" the surface of rocks. With a source of water, can live for weeks without food.
Locomotion: Has tentacles used for locomotion. Follows mucus trails laid by other snails to prevent it from bumping into things.
Reproduction: Is dioecious, but sexes are indistinguishable. Fertilization occurs internally. Females lay eggs directly into the sea. Larvae are planktonic. Eggs: laid in floating capsules, round, pink, 70-84 micrometers wide, laid 700-2,000 at a time. Mating occurs mostly in spring and summer.
Etymology: *Littorina planaxis* (L. *Littoralis* of or belonging to the shore; L. *planus* level, flat; L. *axis* axle, pivot.)
Other: Commercially used for food in European countries such as France. Protect themselves by "gluing" themselves to rocks, effectively sealing the entrance to their shell and retaining moisture in dry, sunny areas.

SCALED WORM SHELL *Serpulorbis squamigerus*

Class *Gastropoda* | **Order** *Heterogastropoda* | **Family** *Architectonicacea*
Morphology: The distal end of the scaled worm shell houses its tentacles. The worm has a whitish, pinkish and yellow tinge to it. The shell curves around and there are a few of them on top of each other.
Range: Mostly live on humid rocky environments on the sea floors or in fresh seawater. They attach to algae, kelp, shells, rocks and below low tide lines. Most commonly seen in California, along the Pacific coast and central Baja California.

Feeding: Are sessile, therefore dependent on water currents to bring them food. They feed by entrapping food particles, bacteria, and minerals present in sea water in their mucous threads and nets.
Reproduction: The females lay massive amounts of fertilized eggs, sometimes over 600 that are placed in about 67 capsules during the summer season. Almost all the eggs in the capsules hatch, releasing swimming larvae. These larvae move around and attach themselves to a rock or tubes of an adult, developing a shell around their body.
Etymology: *Serpulorbis sqamigerus* (L. Serp worm *L. squamigerus* Shell).
Other: Japanese name is Mimizugai, *Serpulorbis squamigerus* .

NAVANAX *Navanax inermis*

Class *Gastropoda* | **Order** *Cephalaspidea* | **Family** *Aglajidae*
Morphology: Fully grown, at least 22 cm in length, dark brown to black with yellow lines going lengthwise up and down the body; edges of the creatures have an orange to yellow line extending all along edge. A series of bright blue spots also fringes the edges.

Range: East Pacific, North America, and West Atlantic Ocean.
Feeding: Feeds on other sea slugs, bubble snails and occasionally nudibranchs. Sucks in the prey, and then swallows repeatedly which moves the prey into the esophagus. The empty shell is then expelled out the other end of the creature.
Locomotion: Uses radial mussels to suck water in from its front and pushes it out its back.
Reproduction: They are all hermaphrodites. The penis is on the right side of the head, with the genital opening being on the right side of the body in the rear, the creature acting as male approaches the female from behind and attaches. Chains can form with 3-6 creatures on average, the creatures in the middle act as both male and female simultaneously.
Etymology: *Navanax inermis* (L. *Navanax*- not, L. *arma* arms, "unarmed").
Other: To feed on snails, it has learned to follow the slime trail that the snails leave in their wake.

DORID NUDIBRANCH
Gymnodoris ceylonica

Order: *Nudibrancha* | **Suborder**: *Doridina* | **Family**: *Gymnodoridae*

Morphology: Their mantles cover their entire dorsal surface and cover their "feet." Their retractable gills are located on the posterior area of the body. Their sensory tentacles located at the head of the animal provide visual and sensory indications, and have a partial shell that covers the top of their bodies.
Range: Found in most cool intertidal locations around the world.
Feeding: Are known to eat soft corals, and anemones, which gives them their toxic makeup; sometimes eat fish eggs, worms, and sea plants.
Locomotion: Uses strands of muscles contracting in order to propel itself along the ocean floor.
Communication: None.
Reproduction: Nudibranchs are hermaphroditic, making it much easer to find a fertile mate. After reproducing the Nudibranch lays a cluster of eggs next to its food source. The eggs mature from 5-50 days, in which they start life in the larval stage, eating plankton and are at the mercy of the currents.
Etymology: (naked gilled partial shell) unknown.

CALIFORNIA SEA HARE
Aplypsia californica

Class: *Gastropoda* | **Order**: *Opisthobranchia* | **Family**: *Aplysiidae*
Morphology: Large, soft, bulky slugs that have tiny little tentacles which somewhat re-semble rabbit ears; lack a head shield which makes them different from other members of their class; usually about 5-16 inches long but some can grow up to 75 cm; weigh 30lbs on average.
Range: Most of the Californian coast and parts of the Gulf of California.
Feeding: Herbivorous; diet consists of red/brown seaweed.
Locomotion: Jet propulsion; move by water being brought into mantle cavity and squeezed out siphon.
Reproduction: Hermaphroditic, generally lay eggs at the end of life; mate in large groups; lay up to 80 million eggs.

Etymology: *Alypsia californica* ("without a shield," Gr. *Aplysia* – a dirty sponge; L. *californica* – of California)
Other: Valuable laboratory animal, used to study neurobiology in relation to learning and memory due to its less complex nervous system composed of unusually large neurons; lifetime depends on water temperature; when threatened, sea hares release a dark purple fluid for defense; sea hares can only distin-guish light from dark.

BAY MUSSEL *Mytilus edulis*

Class: *Pelecypoda* | **Order**: *Mytiloida* | **Family**: *Mytilidae*
Morphology: Composed of two smooth, shiny, bluish-black shells with a long rounded triangular shape that are 6-10 cm long and 3-5 cm high.
Range: Arctic Ocean to Baja California, West Coast of South America, Japan, Australia, North-Atlantic often found on rocks and mussel beds at low tide.
Feeding: They feed submerged at high tide; open shells and use cilia attached to gills to propel water and food particles in mouth. Active suspension feeder on organic particulates and dissolved organic matter. *M. edulis* is a filter feeder capable of removing particles down to 2-3 μm with 80-100% efficiency.
Reproduction: Is not hermaphrodite. During the reproductive phase mantle changes in aspect according to its sex. During reproduction the males and females release their gametes in the sea. Reproductive output size and location is also influenced by temperature, food supply and tidal exposure.
Etymology: *Mytilus edulis* (L. *Mytilus* a sea mussel, L. *edulis* means edible).

PACIFIC OYSTER
Crassostrea gigas

Class: *Bivalvia* | **Order**: *Ostreoida* | **Family**: *Ostreidae*
Morphology: Shell can grow up to 300 mm long, and have varied shapes depending on where the oyster lives. Bivalve; the lower valve is usually cupped and cemented to some hard substrate, while the upper valve or shell is flat and is used to cover and protect the animal living inside. Cupped and flat shapes are on the inner surface of the shell; outer surface is fluted/rough. Outside is chalky tan or white with purple streaks.
Locomotion: In larval stage, oysters use their flagella to swim throughout the ocean.
Range: Introduced species, originating from Japan. Appears from British Columbia to Southern California. Adults are cemented in place, cannot move.
Feeding: This organism feeds off of planktonic algae and mixed phytoplankton of *Isochrysis galbana, pavlova lutheri, Chaetoceros gracilis,* and *Tetraselmis teterathele.*
Reproduction: The spawning of Pacific oysters all depends on a rise in the waters temperature above eighteen degrees Celsius. When spawning takes place, it occurs during the months of July and August. Eggs develop to embryos in 6 hours at 26°C, to trochophore within 12 hours, and to straight hinge larvae within 18 hours.
Etymology: *Crassostrea gigas* (*Crass* L. Thick; *Ostrea* Gk. Oyster; *gigas* L. Giant)
Other: They develop first as males, and after a year begin to function as females.

MOSSY CHITON
Mopalia muscosa

Class: *Polyplacophora* | **Order**: *Neoloricata* | **Family**: *Lepidochitonidae*

Morphology: Up to 2 3⁄4" in length. Eight plates colored gray or black. The girdle is covered with stiff hairs.
Range: Range between Alaska and Baja California; is found in the mid-tidal range; have a home range of only 20".
Feeding: Stay motionless until nightfall when it then feeds on algae.
Locomotion: Uses its muscular foot to move at very slow speeds.
Reproduction: Usually gregarious during times of breeding, while the female takes in the sperm from the males in the water it also uses for respiration.
Etymology: *Mopalia muscosa* (; Italian *muscosa,* mossy)
Other: Usually stay wedged in tight spaces between rocks and never move. They can be identified by their color, skirt, and/or number of segments.

TWO-SPOTTED OCTOPUS
Octopus bimaculoides

Class: *Cephalopoda* | **Order**: *Octopoda* | **Family**: *Octopodidae*
Morphology: Has two bluish eye-like spots on head. Can grow to 30 feet long from top of head to tip of tentacles. Four pairs of tentacles connected with webbing and hundreds of suckers on each sit below a membranous sack that contains most of its major organs.
Range: Common around most intertidal and subtidal zones of western coast of the U.S. and Baja California. Live under rocks and tight spaces where protected from predators.
Feeding: Feeds on mollusks, crustaceans, fishes. Uses tentacles and suckers to latch onto prey and drag towards their hard beaks. Inject toxins through posterior salivary glands upon bite to paralyze prey. Suckers can pry open shells to get to insides.
Locomotion: Can crawl by using tentacles as legs. Large mantle can suck in water which is forced out through siphon to act as a jet.
Reproduction: Females lay eggs under rocks from late winter until summer. The female will then devote her life if necessary to protect her eggs. Many octopi's devotion to protecting their eggs go as far as not hunting or eating to remain close to their nest. Many times the demand of producing a nest of offspring is the last thing a female octopus does in her life.
Etymology: *Octopus bimaculoides* (Gr. *Okto*, eight; *pous*, footed; *bimaculoides*, two spotted).

ANNELIDA

ANNELIDA

The name *Annelida* comes from the Latin word *annelus,* which means "ringed worm." There are two major marine classes of the phylum *Annelida: Hirudinia* and *Polycheata. Hirudinia* contains 520 species of leeches; most are freshwater with a few marine and terrestrial species. They have a fixed number of segments, usually 34. They have posterior and anterior suckers.

Polycheata contains 5000 species, making it the largest class. Members have bristles that allow them to wriggle and move. Since there are an abundance of polychaets, they are a significant part of the marine food chain. They have a well developed head. They do not have clitella, permanent sex organs, or permanent ducts for sex cells. Fertilization is external. Annelids have a segmented body, and bilateral symmetry. The segments are separated by septa. They have a head and a terminal anus and a complete digestive tract (which is non-segmented). They have a nervous system with lateral nerves in each segment. Their major organ systems are closed. They have a segmental-arranged circulatory system with a digestive system composed of a complete tube from mouth to anus. Gas exchange is performed by diffusion through the skin. Certain types of annelids (mainly leeches) are used for medical purposes.

In the San Diego Bay, annelids are commonly found on mud flats. Two of the families of annelids we found in the San Diego bay are the *Cirratulidae* family and the *Nereididae* family. The *Cirratulidae* comes from the order *Cirratulida.* They are deposit feeders that gather their food from the ocean floor. The *Nereididae* are usually large elongated worms with jaws.

CIRRATULIDAE

Class *Polychaete* | **Order** *Canalipalpata* | **Family** *Cirratulidae*
Morphology: Usually red or orange gelatinous covering. Front end of body has a pair of thick grooved palps and tentacular filaments. Some with anterior ends with several grooved tentacular filaments arranged in a transverse row. Visible palps and long thread-like gills. 40-150 mm in length. Some with slender tentacles of two lengths and heavy black spines protruding from sides of body from middle to end.
Habitat: Shallow water and deep sea. Holes and crevices in rocky tidepools, mussel beds, among roots of surfgrass, rocky and soft bottoms, bays and harbors.
Range: California, Baja California, Oregon, British Colombia.
Feeding: Deposit feeders.
Locomotion: Little bristles or tentacles help them wiggle through the sand. Some are able to burrow through rocks or coral using their jaws.
Reproduction: Reproduce asexually by severed body parts, and sexually by external fertilization. Some spawning occurs in Alatimos Bay in Los Angeles during May and June.
Etymology: Scissor-tailed.

NEREIDIDAE

Class: *Polychaeta* | **Order:** *Phyllodocida* | **Family:** *Nereididae*

Morphology: Two pairs of antennae, a pair of bi-articulate palps, a pair of jaws and many paragnaths. Enlarged peristominium forms a collar around the prostomium. Greatly elongated peristomial cirri. Can be anywhere from 70 mm to 1 meter.

Range: British Colombia, California, Siberian Pacific, Mexico, Peru, Hawaii, Japan, China, Australia.

Feeding: Some feed on algae by catching pieces as they float by and attaching them to the walls of their habitat to grow. Some feed on sessile animals.

Locomotion: Bristles are used to wiggle through sand. Jaws are used to burrow through rock. Certain species can swim up to 80 mm per second.

Reproduction: Reproduce asexually by severed body parts, and sexually by external fertilization.

Etymology: A sea nymph.

Other: Often used as bait for fishermen.

ARTHROPODA

ARTHROPODA

The phylum *Arthropoda* contains some of the most prolific animals on the planet. The word arthropoda was derived around 1877. The biology definition, "those with joined feet," meaning the invertebrates' legs are segmented, came about in 1845 by a German scientist. Arthropods can be found in the air, on land, or in the sea. They have the ability to survive in any condition ranging from extreme temperature to extreme toxicity levels. The arthropods make up three-fourths of all known living fossils and organisms. There are over one million species total in this phylum. There are ten important marine classes within this phylum. These important marine classes are T*rilobite* (these are extinct creatures), *Tardigrada, Onychophora, Sprigginida, Vendiamorpha, Anomalocarida, Pycnogonida, Uniramia, Crustaceamorpha,* and *Cheliceramorpha.*

There are so many different kinds of arthropods that it is difficult to define an arthropod. One characteristic that helps define an arthropod is that they have segmented bodies. They can be segmented internally and externally. The segmented parts of an arthropod usually include a head, thorax, and abdomen. Their exoskeleton is composed of chitin which is a strong, flexible, modified polysaccharide. Arthropods have a complete digestive system and a complex nervous system. They have an open circulatory system and a respiration system.

The arthropod's ability to shed or molt is a unique characteristic of this phylum. Arthropods shed because their bodies are segmented which blocks growth of the organism. Shedding allows the arthropod to have rapid growth in size and significant change to the body until a new exoskeleton is made. During shedding, an arthropod is at the highest risk of attack because there is no hard exoskeleton to protect it from enemies.

Throughout all our studying at numerous locations, we have seen many arthropods. We have seen the molt of a lobster. We have also encountered and seen countless numbers of barnacles (*Balanus*). We have also seen another kind of barnacle (*Cthamalus*). We have also seen tons of shore crabs (*Pachygrapsus*) which vary a lot in size. Two other common creatures we saw were rock louse *(Ligia)*, and burrowing shrimp (*Callianassa*). There are many arthropods in and around the bay and these are just a handful of the ones out there.

STRIPED BARNACLE
Balanus amphitrite

Class: *Maxillopoda* | **Order**: *Thoracica* | **Family**: *Balanidae*
Morphology: Small, conical. 15cm in diameter, white with purple or brown stripes running along their shell. Have terga; two pairs of plates surround mouth barnacle. Have labrum, lip-like extension anterior to the mouth.

Range: Throughout the main Hawaiian Islands, Southwestern Pacific and Indian Ocean. Also around world-wide, in warm and temperate seas.
Feeding: Barnacles have specialized paired appendages, called cirri, which they use as a scoop net, reaching out into the water and extracting food particles. When the cirri are drawn back, food is scraped off into the mouth.
Locomotion: Larvae search the substrate with their antennae. When a suitable site has been found they release a substance that fastens to the site. Barnacles live only in marine environments, and many live in intertidal regions. Spend part of their day without seawater. Net of six pairs of long legs and cirri protrudes from the cavity, sweeps through sea water to filter microscopic planktonic cells for food.
Reproduction: Hermaphrodites; cross-fertilization occurs in dense populations. Males deposit sperm into mantle cavity of adjacent functional females via a long tube. Fertilized eggs brooded in mantle cavity; several months before the free-swimming planktonic larvae released.
Etymology: *Balanus amphitrite* (L. *Balanus*, Striped; L. *Amphitrite*, barnacle).

RED GHOST SHRIMP
Callianassa californica

Class: *Crustaceans* | **Order**: *Decapoda* | **Family**: *Callianassidae*

Morphology: Soft-bodied crustaceans that have a long and flexible abdomen. Usually have two chelipeds; males have one cheliped that is larger than the other. At the end of these chelipeds are sharp pinchers. The second leg has long seta, or hairs. Colors range from pale pink to orange. Male shrimp are approximately three inches long and females are two inches long.
Range: Found in mostly muddy areas, but can be found anywhere from muddy shores to the deep sea. They are especially common in the tropics.
Feeding: As the mud passes through digestive tract while digging, they take in organic detritus and microorganisms. Plankton and detritus also provide nutrients that are carried by the water current moving through the burrow. The nutrient is collected by pleopods. Also collect detritus using the fine hairs on its legs. When the hairs collect the food, the third maxilliped takes up the food and delivers it to the mouth.
Reproduction: Females carry young eggs under the pleopods on the abdomen. When eggs hatch, larva swim around for weeks until they settle to make burrows of their own.
Etymology: *Callianassa californiensis*; the genus *Callianassa* comes from Greek mythology and refers to one of the fifty Nereids or sea nymphs renowned for their beauty and kindness.

STRIPED SHORE CRAB   *Pachygrapsus crassipes*

Class: *Malacostraca* | **Order**: *Decapoda* | **Family**: *Grapsidae*
Morphology: Ranges from 3-4cm in width. Has a center body, eight legs, and two front pinchers to defend itself or gather prey. Body is encased in a hard exoskeleton. During the molt it's incredibly soft and vulnerable to predators. Able to retain water in a convenient gill chamber which allows them to stay on land for extended periods of time. Travels to water to gather food and moisten their gills.

Range: Located in Charleston, Oregon; Isla de Santa Margarita, Baja California; Korea, Japan, and the Gulf of California. Tend to live in higher tide pools or crevices.

Feeding: Feed on film from algae as well as eating dead matter, limpets, snails, hermit crabs, and sometimes isopods. Cannibalism can occur with recently molted crabs.

Locomotion: Move by walking side to side on legs. Sometimes use their claws, but usually left in the air to scare off predators. Some use pinchers to dig holes into the sand to hide.

Reproduction: Mate right after the female has molted in summer. The male turns on back and female crawls on top of it. Female later creates a cavity in the sand and lays eggs. Eggs attach to female's legs and she carries them around for several months.

Etymology: *Pachygrapsus crassipes* (Gr. *Pachy*, thick; L. *graspus*, crab; Gr. *Crassipes*, thick foot).

ROCK LOUSE   *Ligia occidentalis*

Class: *Crustacea* | **Order:** *Isopoda* | **Family:** *Ligiidae*
Morphology: Usually grey with orange-tipped legs. Resembles a cockroach. Separated eyes, gills, pointed legs, antennae, forked tail and a moist but rough outer shell.
Communication: A hissing type noise.

Range: Sonoma County, California to San Francisco, California and Central America.
Feeding: Scavengers and scrapers. Feeds on dead plant and animal material. Also on the algal film located on intertidal rocks.
Locomotion: It is able to scurry under different rocks at a fast moving speed.
Reproduction: Separate sexes and sexual reproduction. Spawns from spring to early summer.
Etymology: *Ligia occidentalis* (L. *Ligia*- To fall down or to go down ; L. *occidentalis*- western sky or part of the sky)
Other: Most active at night. Changes its color each morning to become darker during daylight. A terrestrial species. Must live near a water source such as a tide pool. Dips its rear end, located at the gills, into water in order to keep its breathing apparatus moist.

CHORDATA

CHORDATA

We are surrounded by different communities of species in various ecological systems. How biotic and abiotic factors interact with each other determines the ecological separation of species. There are two major ecosystems: terrestrial and aquatic (which includes both salt and freshwater). Of these two ecosystems, chordates can be widely found in either one. *Chordate* is the common name for species of the *Chordata* phylum. The word *Chordata* comes from the Latin word *chorda* and Greek word *chorde* which means *chord*. This gives its species the logical explanation that they have vertebrates. Though a large percentage, approximately 97%, of the 50,000 living chordates are vertebrates, not all are vertebrates. With the wide range of species that this phylum has, there is great diversity.

The most important factor to consider about chordates is how they are developed at the most fundamental level. Chordates are deuterostomes, meaning that they have two mouths. They do not use only one opening for both intake of food and nutrients and decanting of waste products. Chordate cells, beginning at the blastula state, form an opening. As the opening enlarges in the gastrula stage, the opening becomes known as the blastopore. Usually, more primitive phyla like the *Platyhelminthes* and *Coelenterata* do not go any further than this. However, chordate advances in embryology where the blastopore goes all the way through the blastula, forming two openings. Hence, they have an opening for intake and a separate opening for secretion of waste products produced by their internal system. Every chordate is considered to have four anatomical features in their lifetime.

At some point in a chordate's life, it has four main features that may or may not exist later on in its development stage. These include notochord, dorsal hollow nerve cord, pharyngeal slits, and post-anal tail. After gastrulation, organs begin to develop in chordate embryos. Once the mesoderm is formed in the gastrula stage to become the dorsal side of the chordate embryo, the notochord starts to take form. The notochord is sandwiched between the digestive system and the dorsal hollow nerve cord. It is made up of cartilage and is a long, semi-rigid, rodlike structure. The cartilage is made up of stiff fibrous tissues, containing fluid-filled cells. Invertebrate chordates use the notochord in both their embryonic and adult stages for side-to-side movements. Physical support from the notochord enables invertebrate chordates to move through the water. Unlike the invertebrate chordates, vertebrate chordates do not retain their notochord, but replace it with a backbone. The development of the dorsal hollow nerve cord occurs at the same time as the notochord.

Located on top and parallel to the notochord is the dorsal hollow nerve cord. The dorsal hollow nerve cord is formed from a plate of the dorsal ectoderm layer, above the notochord. Two edges of the dorsal ectoderm plate fold inward. When the two edges meet each other, they form a hollow tube. Once the dorsal hollow nerve cord comes off of the ectoderm plate, it then forms the nervous system. Cells located at the site where the dorsal hollow nerve cord meet, migrate to surround the nerve cord. These are responsible for forming other organs such as bones and muscles. The dorsal hollow nerve cord consists of nerve fibers linking the brain to lateral muscles and other organs. These nerve fibers run down the back part of the organism. In most adult chordates, the posterior cells of the dorsal hollow nerve cord forms a spinal cord. The anterior cells of the dorsal hollow nerve cord form a brain.

The third key anatomical feature of all chordates are the pharyngeal slits. The pharyngeal slits are often considered as gills, but are not always used as gills. They are openings, located in the pharynx, just behind the mouth. The inside of the throat is connected to the outside of the neck region through these slits. Chordates perhaps inherited this from their deuterostome ancestor. Invertebrate chordates, like their deuterostome ancestors, use the gills as adults to strain food from the water. For some vertebrates, like fishes, the pharyngeal slits develop into internal gill slits. These vertebrates use the gill slits for gas exchange during respiration.

The fourth and final character of chordates is the post-anal tail. Generally supported and linked to the notochord is the post-anal tail. It is located in the back of the anal opening and extends outward. Muscles that make up the post-anal tail are blocks of modified body segments. This makes it possible for chordates to move through their environment. Humans belong in with chordates because of the post-anal tail during the embryonic stage. However, as development continues, the post-anal tail begins to disappear.

Though the *Chordata* phylum contains a great deal of species, there are four main subphyla that classify these species. These four subphyla include *Myxini, Urochordata, Cephalochordata,* and the most commonly known *Vertebrata.* The *Myxini* used to be thought of as vertebrates, but instead of having a backbone, they have a cranium or skull. Therefore, their group has been renamed to *Craniata,* which encompasses chordates that have a cranium. For the remaining three, their names are unchanged.

The *Urochordata,* consisting of Tunicata, is a marine group commonly known as sea squirts. The young in this subphylum are referred to as larva. For movement, they utilize their tail. However, as they become more mature, they begin to lose their tail and other chordate features. The *Urochordata* then becomes a sack with two siphons. Their only feature that makes these sea squirts chordates are their gill slits. Water is able to enter and exit through the opening of the sack, enabling the *Urochordata* to obtain food. Reproduction occurs asexually, sexually, or hermaphroditically.

Cephalochordata has the species *amphioxus* or lancelets. They have a short tapered body, enabling them to swim. They do not have complex sense organs. *Amphioxuses* are known as sand burrowers because they bury themselves in shallow subtidal or in porous intertidal sand for most of their life time, with their head being exposed to the water. They rarely leave their burrow to swim. Using their tentacles, food is brought into their mouth. They also have separate sexes and their gametes are released into the water when they reach maturity. Throughout their life, the *amphioxuses* keep all of their chordate features.

Vertebrata, or vertebrates, has a diverse number of species from fishes to amphibians and mammals. All the species in this subphylum have a vertebra. The vertebra runs along the dorsal surface from head to tail. Most of the vertebrates have a jaw, except for lampreys, and are referred to as the *Gnathostomata.* About 42 to 400 million years ago, this was the opposite, where there were more jawless vertebrates than there were jawed ones. Some of the unique characteristics of the vertebrates include their extrinsic eye muscles which allow eye movements, ventral heart with 2-4 chambers, well developed body cavity, and integument of two divisions.

The phylum *Chordata* is a vastly diverse phylum. It contains much of the life forms that everyone is familiar with and is highly adaptive in various environments around the world. Within the San Diego Bay there are many different chordates of birds, ducks, raptors, fish, and mammals. Some of the birds found in San Diego Bay area include eared-grebes, willets, great blue herons, lesser blue herons, snowy egrets, and belted kingfishers. Ducks seen in San Diego Bay include American coots, northern pintails, and redhead ducks. Types of fish in the Bay include topsmelt, northern clingfish, tidepool sculpin, and spotted bay bass. Raptors and mammals found in the Bay were red-shouldered hawks, ospreys, bottlenose dolphins, California sea lions, and ground squirrels.

UROCHORDATA

Urochordata is a sub-phylum of the phylum *Chordata,* a phylum characterized by a notochord, post-anal tail, pharyngeal slits, and hollow dorsal nerves. Often known as sea squirts or tunicata, Urochordates seem to be simple creatures at first glance. Often found immobile and affixed to objects, they are easily mistaken as Cnidaria by the casual observer. Urochordates are split into three groups, *Ascidiacea, Thaliacea,* and *Appendicularia.*

The most common sub-branch of *Urochordata* is *Ascideiacea.* Retaining the characteristics of chordata only through their larval stages, *Ascideiacea* have a great metamorphosis when becoming adults. First, they lose their post-anal tail, reducing their body to only their head. This head attaches itself to a rock by its mouth and turns into an immobile filter feeder. Much like a basket, the mature *Ascideiacea* just stays on a rock or other hard object and pulls water into its stomach.

Thaliacea colonies can be described as amazing to say the least. Grouping together to create colonies longer than a meter in length, Thaliacea float around the ocean all their life. Like most *Urochordates, Thaliacea* filter feed plankton through their barrel-shaped bodies. They also use the shape of their body to shoot water out for propulsion. *Appendicularia,* also called *Larvacea,* are the most unique out of *Urochordata*'s three sub-branches. Free-floating like their brothers, the *Thaliacea, Appendicularia* set themselves apart through their structure and feeding habits. In the larval stage, *Appendicularia* looks much like a tadpole. Possessing all the characteristics of the phylum *Chordata, Appendicularia* does not lose these as they develop into adults. As adults, the tail becomes perpendicular to the head. *Appendicularia* improves upon its filter feeding by creating a mechanism close to that of a fishing net. The *Appendicularia* creates a shell made of protein and cellulose that attract food. The shell over time gets saturated with food and the *Appendicularia* eats the saturated food. In a sense, *Appendicularia* is the most advanced out of *Urochordata*'s three sub-branches. They have more advanced eating habits and retain the characteristics of phylum *Chordata* throughout their lives.

TUNICATE
Steyela clava

Class: *Ascidiacea* | **Order**: *Pleurogona* | **Family**: *Styelidae*

Morphology: Long narrow body, length up to 15 cm. Leathery surface. 2-4 gonads on left side and 5-8 on right each with an ovary surrounded by male follicles. Can reproduce sexually or asexually.

Range: Rocks, floats, pilings, low intertidal zones, usually in calm waters. Found in San Francisco Bay to San Diego Bay, Japan, Asian mainland, Austrailia, northwestern European harbors, northeastern United States. Attach to boats and are transported everywhere. Attach to man-made structures and rocks in shallow water.

Feeding: Filter feeders

Locomotion: Only moves once in its life. In larval state, swims using its small tail to select preferred habitat.

Reproduction: Can reproduce sexually or asexually. 2-4 gonads on left side and 5-8 on right each with an ovary surrounded by male follicles.

Etymology: *Styela clava* (L. *Styela* herdman; L. *clava* club)

Other: Tunicate blood contains high concentrations of the rare metal vanadium.

BONY FISH

BONY FISH

The class *Osteichthyes* includes all bony fishes. Like all fishes, *Osteichthyes* are cold-blooded vertebrates that breathe through gills and use fins for swimming. Bony fishes share several distinguishing features: a skeleton of bone, scales, paired fins, one pair of gill openings, jaws, and paired nostrils. The class *Osteichthyes* has the largest number of scientific classes of vertebrates; there are more than 23,599 species included. The *Osteichthyes* account for about 96% of all fish species. Some species of fish that are not included in the *Osteichthyes* are the *Chondrichthyes* (sharks and their relatives), the *Myxini* (hagfishes), and the *Cephalaspidomorphi* (lampreys). Living *Osteichthyes* are divided into three subclasses: *Dipnoi, Crossopterygii,* and *Actinopterygii.*

Bony fishes are found in almost every body of water. They are found in tropical, temperate, and polar seas. Bony fishes live in fresh water, seawater, and brackish environments. Some species of bony fishes live as deep as 11 km (6.8 mi.) in the great depths of the oceans. Other species inhabit lakes as high as 5 km (3.1 mi.) above sea level (Lagler, 1962). Approximately 58% of all species of bony fishes live in marine environments. Freshwater fishes make up approximately 42% of fish species. Some species of bony fishes aren't limited to one particular environment. Diadromous bony fish species migrate between fresh and brackish environments. Food, space, reproduction, environmental cycles, and temperature change are some of the main causes of migration for some species.

Most bony fishes have a spindle-shaped (rounded and tapering at both ends) body shape. This body shape reduces drag and requires a very small amount of energy to swim. Bony fish forms an angle from the fusiform body shape in three directions: compression, depression, and elongation.

A laterally compressed body shape is common in bony fishes that live in dense cover or within coral reefs. The compressed body is laterally flattened. Butterfly fishes (family *Chaetodontidae*) are good examples of bony fishes with a laterally compressed body shape.

TOPSMELT   *Atherinops affinis*

Class: *Osteichthyes* | **Order:** *Atheriniformes* | **Family:** *Atherinidae*
Morphology: Dorsal fin, anal fin, pectoral fin, mouth, vertebrae.
Range: Extends from the Gulf of California to Vancouver.
Feeding: Individuals in estuaries eat plant material, small crustaceans, polychaetes, and gastropods. Individuals in the oceans eat planktonic crustacean carnivores, mysids, ostracods, copepods, crustacean larvae.
Reproduction: External fertilization.
Etymology: *Atherinops affinis* (L. *Atherinops* small spiny-finned fishes; L. *affinis* resemblance).

TIDEPOOL SCULPIN
Oligocottus maculosos

Class: *Actinopterygii* | **Order**: *Scopaeniformes* | **Family**: *Cottidae*
Morphology: Range in color from brown to green or red. Have lighter undersides and are capable of changing color to match the environment. Reach up to 3 inches long. Have a single spine towards the front of their head that is forked at the tip.
Range: Bering Sea south to Southern California, as well as the Sea of Okhotsk in Russia.
Feeding: Eat small crustaceans and fish eggs.
Locomotion: Sculpin use their fins and tail to swim. Have two pectoral fins to steer. The tail fin is used for propulsion. If a sculpin is swept away from its tide pool, it has the capability to find its original living space.
Reproduction: Sculpin males have multiple partners during one season. Males will guard eggs until they hatch.
Etymology: *Oligocottus maculosos* (G. *Oligos*: small, little; G. *kottos*: a kind of fish; L. *maculare:* to make spotted)/

NORTHERN CLINGFISH
Gobiesox maeandricus

Class: *Actinopterygii* | **Order:** *Perciformes* | **Family:** *Gobiesocida*
Morphology: Can grow to 6", or 16 cm, in length. Color varies from light olive brown to cherry red mottled with dark brown. Have white bars between eyes and, in juveniles, going across the back and edge of the caudal fin. Have dark radiating lines joining eyes through a series of reticulations.
Belly has a large circular adhesive disc, which is separated from fins by a notch. This supports the fish and allows them to be flexible. Caudal fins are rounded; pectoral fins are short and broad, and pelvic fins are united by a papillose membrane. Have a fleshy pulp between the base of the fin and gill opening.
Range: Southeast Alaska to Mexico. Usually found under rocks from intertidal to sub-tidal zones where tidal currents are strong.
Feeding: The northern clingfish feeds off the ocean floor; it predominately eats small crustaceans. Specifically, it is cannibalistic and eats sculpins and smaller northern clingfish, as well as small crustaceans and mollusks such as white-lined chiton, lined chiton, shield limpet, plate limpet, ribbed limpet, mask limpet, red rock crab.
Locomotion: Using its scrawny fins, the northern clingfish swims through the water.
Reproduction: The northern clingfish lays eggs in the spring.
Etymology: *Gobbiesox maeandricus* (L. *Gobius* Gudgeon; L. *Esox* Pike; G. *maeandros* Circuitous Windings.)
Other: Breathes air when out of water. The only commercial use is their inclusion in public aquariums.

SPOTTED BAY BASS
Paralabrax maculatofasciatus

Class: *Teleostei* | **Order:** *Perciformes* | **Family:** *Serranidae*
Morphology: Characterized by an overall yellowish-tan color, covered with numerous orange, black and brown spots that coalesce to form mottled bars on its sides. The belly is white, and the third dorsal spine is elongated, about three times longer than the second dorsal spine.
Range: Abundant along the Pacific side of the Baja California peninsula, throughout the Sea of Cortez south to Punta Chivato, and along the coast of mainland north of Guaymas.
Feeding: Feeds on anything that will fit into its mouth.
Locomotion: Uses its tail as means of locomotion to swim through waters; uses fins as means of steering.
Reproduction: Occurs near southern California embayments from June through August. Spotties lay pelagic (floating) eggs which enter plankton in coastal waters.
Etymology: *Paralabrax macula* (L. *Macula* Lighting or fiery meteor).

AVES

AVES: DUCKS AND GEESE

The most noticeable creatures of the San Diego Bay are perhaps those representing class *Aves*. There are over 8 to 10 thousand living bird species in the world, and if you've ever been down by the Bay during the spring and summer months, you'd say that you've seen about that many loitering around the boardwalks and the beaches. Birds are said to have evolved from theropod dinosaurs and are seen in the wild and in many homes as domesticated pets.

Birds are bipedal, warm-blooded members of the phylum *Chordata*, and they are characterized by being egg-laying, feathered creatures with wings and hollow bones. All possess a bony beak sans teeth, the ability to lay hard-shelled eggs, a very light but still very strong skeleton, and a high metabolic rate. They are known to exhibit many differentiations between each class and species. For example, birds have an immense range in size and can be anywhere from as small as a hummingbird to as large as the ostrich or emu. Most are diurnal, but some, like owls, are nocturnal. Many migrate long distances to switch between habitats during season changes, whereas others stay in one place their entire lives, and others still are completely unable to fly anywhere. Eating habits also vary from species to species. Some are more inclined to eat nectar, seeds, and insects, but others prefer to dine on rodents, fish, roadkill, or even other birds.

The phylum *Aves* has an incredible number of taxonomic orders within it. A variety of ducks may be observed around San Diego Bay from November to March. Some of the more common members include the *Anseriformes* (the waterfowl), the *Columbiformes* (doves and pigeons), the *Faconiformes/Accipitriformes* (the raptors), and the *Pelecaniformes* (the pelicans). We saw representatives of some of the other classes of birds as well.

Many of the birds seen around the Bay were members of the *Anatidae* family. These birds are commonly referred to as the ducks. Ducks are mostly aquatic birds that are fairly small and usually found in both fresh and salt water. They eat a variety of different foods including fish, insects, grains, and grasses, though as tourism to San Diego increases with each passing year, the diets of ducks are slowly expanding to include leftovers from many human lunches. Ducks migrate during the fall to warmer climates, and return to their normal habitats in the spring. Ducks are an important part of their ecosystems and food webs, and also serve as an important part of many economies as their meat, eggs, feathers, and down are widely used around the world.

MALLARD

Anas platyrhincus

Class: *Aves* | **Order:** *Anseriformes* | **Family:** *Anatidae*
Morphology: All mallard ducks have a blue speculum on the wings in both sexes. The male or drake characteristics are the green plumage on the head and neck, and curled black feathers on its tail. He will also have a white ring around the neck, dark breast, yellow bill, and orange-red feet. The female or hen's plumage is drab brown. She has an orange bill and feet.
Communication: They range from mating, inciting, and social calls. The volume of its call will increase as nervousness and anxiety climb. The pitch will deepen as the mallard gets larger and the duration will increase. The all-known "quack" is given by the female to call in her ducklings to her and it can be heard for miles.
Range: Roughly the entire world, however mainly the Northern Hemisphere. The species contains the largest breeding range of any bird on the North American Continent. The mallard may have also been the first domesticated bird, springing from it many domestic breeds.
Feeding: They eat vegetation, insects, worms, gastropods and arthropods. They usually feed at the surface of the water and don't dive all the way under.
Locomotion: Mallards, like all puddle ducks, can fly directly into the air without having to run and gain momentum like a diving duck. Mallards will fly in small groups of U or V formations. These groups can consist of the usual 10-20 members or several hundred. Mallards are excellent swimmers and swift fliers.
Reproduction: Most mallards are capable of breeding as yearlings but usually produce fertile offspring as adults. Pair bonding starts as early as October and continues throughout March. The mallard male soon leaves the hen after mating. The hen will then lay about 9 to 13 eggs in a nest on the ground nearby a body of water. The ducklings will hatch after 26 to 28 days, and then the hen will lead them to the water never to return.
Etymology: *Anas platyrhynchos* (L. *Anas* Duck; G. *Platys* broad or flat; G. *rynchos* Beak).

BUFFLEHEAD

Bucephala albeola

Class: *Aves* | **Order:** *Anseriformes* | **Family:** *Anatidae*
Morphology: Hardly reaching 1 pound they are the smallest diving ducks. Male buffleheads have black back and white under,sides, two tone purple and dark green on the neck and head, with a large white patch. Females have brownish backs and grayish undersides, and a black head with white patch on its cheek.
Communication: Squeaks, chatters, growls, and guttural rolls; females make softer sounds.
Range: Any woodland from Alaska to Manitoba, California, Washington, Wyoming, Oregon, Montana, Vermont and Massachusetts.
Feeding: Aquatic insects, crustaceans, small fish, and some vegetation.
Locomotion: Unlike most ducks they don't need to run along the surface of the water in order to fly, and most of their flying is done fast and low.
Reproduction: Pairing occurs during spring migration. Females lay some 7 to 11 eggs, 46mm large. Color range from white to olive green. A typical nest is a tree cavity. Incubation lasts about a month. Hatchlings stay in the nest for another month.
Etymology: *Bucephala albeola* (G, *Cephala* Head; L, *Albeola* White)

GREATER SCAUP
Aythya marila

Class: *Aves* | **Order:** *Anseriformes* | **Family:** *Anatidae*
Morphology: Small compact diving duck. Length: 13 - 17 inches. Weight: 1.5 to 2.0 pounds. Yellow eyes, blue bill with small black nail at tip.
Communication: Utters a soft cooing and whistles notes in courtship. Males make a discordant "scaup" noise; females are silent.
Range: Boreal forests of Canada and wintering grounds in the Atlantic coast and the Great Lakes or migrate offshore from Alaska.
Feeding: Aquatic plants, insects, mollusks, and snails.
Locomotion: Air/underwater movement aided with wings.

Reproduction: Nest is a hollow lined with plant matter and down, often in an open site. Female lays 8 11 olive-buff colored eggs and incubates for 24-28 days. Young are downy; leave the nest soon after hatching and fly at about 5-6 weeks.
Etymology: Perhaps from Scots *scalp, scaup*: bed of mussels (from its feeding on shell-fish).

AMERICAN COOT
Fulica americana

Class: *Aves* | **Order:** *Ralliformes* | **Family:** *Rallidae*
Morphology: Slate gray head, neck, back, upperwings, breast and belly with short wings and a short tail. Very short, thick bill. White bill with dark reddish ring just before tip. White frontal shield with reddish oval near tip.
Communication: Make a wide variety of noises, from grunting to clucking, as a means of communication, between each other and to threatening predators. There are two times a coot will splash: during mating season to attract attention, and to discourage predators.
Range: Migratory birds that during the summer are found in freshwater lakes and ponds of the northern United States (New York and Massachusets) and southern Canada. During winter, they head to the southern portion of the United States and are found from California to Florida.

Feeding: Mostly vegetable matter, including leaves, roots, and seeds of aquatic plants; algae; insects, fish, tadpoles, crustaceans, worms; sometimes, the eggs of other birds.
Locomotion: They float, have webbed feet for speedy, over-water locomotion, have water-proof feathers and insulating down, and some can even use their wings to propel them under water.
Reproduction: The nesting areas or ranges incorporate water, a relaxation spot, nesting cover and food. Nesting- 8-10 pinkish eggs, spotted with brown, on a shallow platform of dead leaves and stems, usually on water but anchored to a clump of reeds. Incubation lasts about 25 days.
Etymology: c.1300, *cote*, used for various water fowl (now limited to *Fulica atra* and, in North America, F. *americana*), of uncertain origin (cf. Du. *meercoet* "lake coot").

BRANT

Branta bernicula

Class: *Aves* | **Order**: *Anseriformes* | **Family**: *Anatidae*
Morphology: Brant are about 60 cm long and
have a short stubby bill. They have a brown/black
body and pure white under tail. They have a white
'necklace' on their neck.
Communication: Quick little squawks.
Range: East and West coast and their migration
range from Alaska and Canada.
Feeding: As adults, they eat mostly eelgrass that
can be found in the San Diego bay.
Locomotion: They fly but because they don't
oil their wings, their flight is much more difficult
than normal birds. They have to flap much more
than normal birds and their flight path is much lower.

Reproduction: Brant females lay between 4-6 eggs on Arctic coastlines. The eggs hatch
after 28 days of incubation. Once the eggs have hatched the male assumes the role of
teaching the birds. At a young age the babies feed on marine invertebrates, mosquito
larvae, and various plants as they mature.
Etymology: Variant of Brent (-goose), possibly from Middle English brende, brindled
Other: In 1931, the eelgrass was killed in most habitats and the Brant was almost wiped
out. Special focuses were made to bring the grass back and the bird is slowly recovering. Brant were first raised in captivity outside of Canada and Alaska by Ron Vavra of El
Cajon in 1973. He did this by recreating the Arctic summer with floodlights on timers.

NORTHERN PINTAIL

Anas acuta

Class: *Aves* | **Order:** *Anseriformes* | **Family:**
Anatidae
Morphology: One of the larger species of duck
and differ vastly in coloration between sexes.
Males have dark brown heads with bright white
chests, grey wings and long dark brown tail
feathers that come to a point, giving the species
its name. Females are different shades of brown
with shorter brown tail feathers.
Communication: Male makes wheezy mewing
notes and a whistle. Female quacks.
Range: The pintail lives mostly on the West
Coast and in the central portion of the United
States and Canada and migrate to lower latitudes
in winter.
Feeding: Pintails are self-sufficient and feed on small invertebrates, gradually adding
plant material to diet such as seeds of grasses, sedges, pondweeds, also vegetative parts.
Locomotion: Flight/walk (immediately after birth)/swim.
Reproduction: Mating begins in April/May.
Females build their nests on the ground usu-
ally in residual cover of short grasses or other
vegetation, in brush, or in the open. Pintails lay
from 6-12 eggs and ducklings hatch together
usually at around 23-24 days.
Etymology: *Anas acuta* (L. *Anas* - Type genus
of the *Anatidae*: freshwater ducks, L. *acuta*
- Sharp or pointed)

COMMON MERGANSER
Mergus merganser

Class: *Aves* | **Order:** *Anseriformes* | **Family:** *Anatidae*
Morphology: Length is 18 inches, wingspan 37 inches. Pointed bill and serrated edges. Red bill is thick with a tapered crest. Red or black head is common. White plumage with dark bar. Alternative plumage in winter and fall months.
Communication: Males have a whistle while female squawks tend to sound like hoarse croaks.
Range: Non breeding season usually brings them to North Pacific habitats. Breeds in North America from central and south-coastal. Winters from the Aleutian Islands and south-coastal Alaska east across southern Canada to Newfoundland and south to southern California and the Gulf Coast.
Feeding: Mostly fish and some invertebrates are ingested.
Reproduction: Monogamous; one mate. Nest is usually placed on existing tree crevices although they can be in various holes or crevices. Eight to eleven eggs are laid and are incubated for 28-35 days. Young stay with female for 65-85 days until fledging.
Etymology: *Mergus Merganser* (L. *Mergus* Sea Bird; L. *Merganser* "waterfowl, diver," from mergere "to dip, immerse")
Other: Due to the wing length and loading time, they must run across the water to take off. When learning to fly, they must sometimes endure a 15 m fall due to the height of nests. Parachuting or fluttering is known to occur.

REDHEADED DUCK
Aythya americana

Order: *Anseriformes* | **Family:** *Anatidae* | **Genus:** *Aythya*
Morphology: 50cm long and 770 grams for males and 680 grams for females. Males have a white crown, blue and black tipped bill, light brown breast, and speckled gray face and neck. Females have a slightly darker crown, pale breast, and a green speculum which is bordered with black.
Communication: Communication is vocal. One of the loudest of diving ducks. When taking off, females let out a loud squawk while males tend to have more of a purr when speaking to each other.
Range: Inhabit in California, and parts of the Great Lakes. Breeding is in Alaska, Central Canada, and Northern United States. During the winter, they can be seen in Southern United States, and Mexico. Known for continually traveling.
Feeding: Eats mainly aquatic vegetation and invertebrates. Favorite animal prey includes snails, crustaceans, and insects. Ducklings eat the same foods as adults.
Locomotion: Can fly as well as swim.
Reproduction: Sexually. They have mating rituals which are also characteristic of the other Aythya species. Females use inciting calls and perform neck stretching. The males then perform the "kinked-neck call" which is similar to a very long slow head throw. Other mating rituals include the "turn the back of the head" display and the "preen behind the wing" display.

Etymology: *Aythya americana.* (L. *Aythya* diving duck species; L. *Americana* America)
Other: Because Redheads eat small, hard food items, they accidentally eat lead bullets mistaking them for food. Large numbers of Redheads die from lead poisoning each year, particularly in Canada, where lead shots have not been particularly banned. In the 1960's and 1970's they had to be protected because of fear of endangerment due to over-hunting. A complete ban was imposed from 1960 to 1963. Only small quotas have been allowed since then.

SURF SCOTER
Melanitta perspicillata

Class: *Aves* | **Sub-class:** *Neornithes* | **Order:** *Anseriformes* | **Family:** *Anatidae*
Morphology: Medium-sized diving duck. The average length is 14 inches while the wingspan is usually around 33 inches. Bill is multicolored with white, red, yellow, and black. It appears mainly orange and is swollen at the base. Females differ with a brown plumage with a slightly paler belly and two indistinct white patches below the eye. Female bill is greenish black.
Communication: Have the ability to vocalize but they are generally silent. Males may make a gurgling or croaking sound during mating rituals.
Range: Breed exclusively in North America. Breeds from Alaska and central British Columbia to the Ungava Peninsula. Winters on the Atlantic coast from Newfoundland to Florida, and on the Pacific coast from the Aleutian Islands to Baja California.
Feeding: Surf Scoters dive to gain food. Diet consists of mussels, small crabs, clams, barnacles and aquatic insects although they do tend to ingest small amounts of sea plants.
Locomotion: A diving duck with the ability to fly.
Reproduction: Sexually. Nests are built around freshwater lakes and are often inland near bushes or immersed aquatic plants. The nest is usually set in a shallow depression in the ground near water. Because of this, scoter nests are one of the hardest to find. Incubation lasts about 28 days and reap an average of five to seven eggs.
Etymology: unknown
Other: San Diego bay supports probably the largest concentration of surf scoters in the species' entire winter range.

PACIFIC FLYWAY

The Pacific Flyway is one of the four major migration routes for migratory birds in the United States, Canada and Mexico. The flight path includes Alaska, Arizona, California, Idaho, Nevada, Oregon, Utah, Washington, and those portions of Colorado, Montana, New Mexico, and Wyoming west of the Continental Divide. The Pacific Flyway starts near the Arctic Archipelago and the eastern base of the Rocky Mountains in Canada. The territory is comprised along the western Arctic, including the Pacific coast regions of Canada, the United States and Mexico, then down south near Central and South America where other flyways blend together.

The flyway includes the passage of gulls, ducks and other water birds that begin their journey in Point Barrow, Alaska and at other points on the Arctic coast. The longest and most important route of the Pacific Flyway is one that originates in northeastern Alaska. Most of the waterfowl that travel the United States section of this route come from Alaska. The Pacific Flyway then closely parallels the eastern foothills of the Rocky Mountains. Near the international border, the route branches and while large flights continue southeastward into the Central and Mississippi flyways, others turn southwestward across northwestern Montana and the panhandle of Idaho, follow along the Snake and Columbia River valleys and then turn southward across central Oregon to the interior valleys of California. Suitable winter quarters for birds are found in California from the Sacramento Valley south to Salton Sea and in the tidal marshes near San Francisco Bay.

The southward route of migratory land birds of the Pacific Flyway that in winter leave the United States extends through the interior of California to the mouth of the Colorado River and on to the winter quarters that are principally in western Mexico.

AVES: SHOREBIRDS

Shorebirds are common throughout San Diego bay. We see them as sandpipers, godwits, yellowlegs, willets, etc. They stay near the land and search through large bodies of water to search for food. They also search in mud and shallow pools. Shorebirds are known to feed on invertebrates such as worms, larvae, clams, snails, etc. Birds with long legs and long beaks stand in somewhat shallow waters and forage for food by sticking their beaks in the water. The birds with smaller spoon-shaped beaks are used to scoop up small fish and other creatures.

They can stay in flight for 70 hours and keep a consistent speed of 50 miles per hour. They can cover over 2,000 miles in one flight. Although their main habitat surrounds the bay, they usually breed and lay eggs in the Arctic. They are a very diverse group on several levels. In size, shorebirds can range from a few ounces to over a pound and a half. Size isn't the only thing they can differ in. Others have a color range that goes from a drab 2 color to a very vibrant array of colors. They molt their feathers twice a year - once in the spring and as they get ready for winter. They molt all of their vibrantly colored feathers in exchange for the more solid and plain colors for the winter time.

The most common threat towards shorebirds is a loss of habitat. More and more land is destroyed in order for construction development and this causes the shorebirds to lose their habitat. This forces the shorebirds to relocate in order to find a suitable place to continue their lives.

WILLET
Cataptrophotus semipalmatus

Class: *Aves* | **Order:** *Charadriiformes* | **Family:** *Scolopacidae*
Morphology: The willet is a large shorebird that appears all gray. But the real giveaway is the black and white pattern on their wings that can only be seen when they're flying. They range from 14-17 inches long with a wingspan of 24-31 ounces. They are gray above, white below, and lightly barred on the flanks. They are large plump-looking long legged shorebirds. The difference between sexes is that the female is slightly larger than the male.
Communication: The willets are usually the loudest bird in their area, especially during their mating and nesting period. When an intruder is spotted an adult will fly circles around the colony or perch on a limb and make its will-will-willet call to alert the others. Aside from using their voice for alerting and protecting, the males also use their voice for courtship or mating, using a kuk-kuk-kuk call to attract the females.
Range: Southern U.S. and East Coast, central to southern Canada, Gulf of Mexico, Southern Nova Scotia, and South America.
Feeding: Will probe for food with bill or snatch it from the ground. Although they are fairly colonial creatures, feeding is done pretty much alone. Willets eat aquatic insects, marine worms, small crabs (fiddlers and hippa crabs), small mollusks, fish, some grasses, tender shoots, seeds and cultivated rice.
Reproduction: Prefer nesting on sandy offshore islands with tall thick grasses, upper coastal beaches, dune edges, flat ground, or high dry places in marshes. They lay four olive-spotted eggs blotched with brown spots from April to May. Incubation is done by the female and sometimes by the male at night. The young will then fly at 22 days of age. The male will also participate in a ceremony by bowing low before exchanging places with her on the nest. This ritual is repeated for 22 days, and after hatch the chicks are free to roam as they please, under parental supervision.
Etymology: unknown.

MARBLED GODWIT
Limosa fedoa

Class: *Aves* | **Order:** *Charadriiformes* | **Family:** *Scolopacidae*
Morphology: Ranges from 16-18 inches tall as an adult. This bird is basically a shorebird that makes it home around San Diego and Tijuana bodies of water. Many of the birds nest with brown material that has a green bottom like grass or other green weeds. The bird has dark upper parts with a light mottled wing pattern. The color of the wing lining is a light brown cinnamon color. The belly is the same. The females have dark brown barring on their breast and flanks.
Communication: They communicate with loud kerrecks.
Range: The birds can be found on grassy plains, salt marshes, tidal creeks, mudflats and sea beaches. Typically the birds are found in Southern California; however, their breeding grounds range from the central plains from Saskatchewan to Minnesota and on coasts from California to Virginia and along the Gulf Coast.
Feeding: The Marbled Godwit feeds typically on small insects that are buried underneath the ground. The Marbled Godwit probes the wet sand and mud with its long bill searching for aquatic invertebrates and small insects. It also eats seeds.
Reproduction: Breeds on grassy plains; visits salt marshes, tidal creeks, mudflats, and sea beaches on migration.
Etymology: unknown.

WESTERN GULL
Larus occidentalis

Class *Aves* | **Order** *Charadriiformes* | **Family** *Laridae*
Morphology: Large gull that is usually 24-27 inches in length. Has a white body, with dark gray wings and back and black wingtips. Has large, bright yellow bills with a red spot, and dark yellow eyes. Feet are usually pinkish or flesh-colored.
Communication: Communicates through squeals and raucous notes.
Range: Can be found near the coast, ranging from Washington to Baja California. They can also be found offshore, on the open ocean. They typically nest on rocky, sandy, or gravel islands, and live in a variety of habitats, such as beaches, harbors, fields, and garbage dumps.
Feeding: They are omnivores and feed in pelagic and intertidal environments. They cannot dive, so they feed exclusively on the surface. They will feed on seal and sea lion corpses, fish, eggs, carrion, and other birds. They will also feed on garbage and steal food from people at marinas and beaches.
Reproduction: Nests in colonies, usually on offshore islands or abandoned piers and cliffs. They will construct a nest of vegetation, often next to a rock or some other object that protects the nest from the wind and hides it from others. The female will usually lay 3 eggs, which are incubated for a month. The chicks generally begin to fly 6 to 7 weeks after hatching, and leave the colony and become independent from their parents after 10 weeks.
Etymology: *Larus occidentalis* (L. *Larus* Ravenous Sea-Bird; L. *occidentalis* Western).

GREAT BLUE HERON
Ardea herodias

Class: *Aves* | **Order:** *Ciconiiformes* | **Family:** *Ardeidae*
Morphology: Males are slightly bigger than females. Usually 46 inches tall with a wingspan of 72 inches. Their plumage is blue-gray with a white head. They also have a heavy, yellow bill.
Communication: Makes a low, heavy, and course grunting quuck (an old rusty car door opening).
Range: Are solitary, but nest communally with hundreds, and are sensitive to the effects of human disturbances. Live in marshes or other wetlands throughout North and Central America. A few will migrate to South America. Locally they nest in trees adjacent to Sea World.
Feeding: Spears its prey with its heavy bill, then throws it into the air and swallows it whole. Prey includes frogs, fish, lizards, snakes, crabs, crayfish, and a variety of insects.
Reproduction: Bonding occurs between mid-February to early April. The females lay between three to seven eggs on a low platform made of sticks and twigs and lined with soft material. The eggs usually hatch in four weeks around late April to early May. It takes the eggs about a month to hatch and the chicks will fledge when they are about two months old.

Etymology: *Ardea herodias* (L. *Ardea*, heron; Gr. *herodias*, heron).

LITTLE BLUE HERON
Egretta caerulea

Class: *Aves* | **Order**: *Ciconiiformes* | **Family**: *Ardeidae*
Morphology: Has blue-gray, black-tipped bill. Has blue-gray belly. Neck usually in S-shape. Has dull, green legs. Long beak makes it easier to catch food. Has a wingspan of 6 ft; much smaller than the great blue heron.
Communication: Makes a sort of "frahnk" noise when speaking.
Range: Lives mostly in North America. Prefers wetlands and swampy areas.
Feeding: Mainly enjoys swiping fish out of the water, but also has a fancy for lizards, frogs and insects.
Reproduction: Nests in platforms of twigs and sticks that are on trees, cliffs, hills, or even on the ground. Female lays 3-7 green eggs at one time.
Etymology: *Egretta caerulea* (Gr. *Egretta* heron; L. *coeruleus*, from coelum sky)
Other: Its long beak makes it easier to catch food. Has a wide wingspan of 6 ft. The heron is easily frightened and is difficult to approach for observation.

SNOWY EGRET
Aigrette thula

Order: *Ciconiiformes* | **Family:** *Ardeidae*
Morphology: Has slender black bill, black legs, and yellow feet. Has long thin legs and a neck that it usually holds in a "S" while flying.
Communication: Has a high and low pitched sound. Snowy Egret makes a "wah-wah-wah" sound.
Range: The Snowy Egret is found in many locations. They are found in the United States and southern Canada. They are found in south Central America, the West Indies, South America and Argentina. They are found along shorelines, coastal areas, swamps and marshes.
Feeding: Usually eats shrimp, minnows, and other small fish. Also feeds on crustaceans, frogs and if you're at Seaworld, they eat churros.
Locomotion: The way this bird gets around is by flying, walking and running.
Reproduction: This bird makes nests in freshwater and saltwater areas. They usually make their nest out of fine twigs.
Etymology: *Egretta Thula* (L. *Egretta*, egret; O.E. *thula*: string of words).

LONG-BILLED CURLEW *Numenius americanus*

Class *Aves* | **Order** *Charadriiformes* | **Family** *Scolopacidae*
Morphology: Curlews are usually brown and beige in color. They have a sickle-shaped bill and a soft tan color decorated in small brown dashes. Their wings have a colorful pattern mixture of brown and light dashes. Females appear slightly larger than the males.
Communication: The curlew's song is inconsistent; it varies going up and down. Their calls are melodious with flute –like notes with vibrations.
Range: The long-billed curlew breeds all over North America. It breeds from southern Canada to northern California, Texas, Utah and Northern Mexico. They are neo-tropical migrators meaning that their food supply is reduced during certain seasons.
Feeding: They feed mainly in grasslands, fields, sometimes in marshes and mudflats during the winter season.
Mostly feed on large marine invertebrates insects such as grasshoppers, beetles and caterpillars. Use their incredibly long bills to pick up food from the ground or probe under the surface of soil.
Reproduction: The reproduction seasons begins around late March and ends in mid July. The males usually attract the females by maneuvering and displaying outstanding flight patterns. The females lay 3-5 five eggs in holes on the ground, near rocks, shrubs or bushes.
Etymology: *Numenius americanus* (L. *Numenius* divine; L. *americanus* American).

SOLITARY SANDPIPER *Tontanus solitariust*

Class: *Aves* | **Order:** *Charadriiformes* | **Family:** *Scolopacidae*
Morphology: Long legs and long, slender bills for probing in the sand or mud for their prey. Plumage is dull, usually streaked brown or gray above and buff with streaks or dark spots below on white feathers.
Communication: A high-pitched peet-weet or peet-weet-weet.
Range: Breeds in Alaska and across Canada to Labrador, south to northeastern Minnesota. Winters in American tropics.
Feeding: Scavengers.
Reproduction: Male incubates 4 eggs (usually) for 20-21 days. Male may change its mate if nest fails. Young are attended by male; they leave the nest soon after hatching, and fly at 13-16 days.
Etymology: *Tringa solitaria* (unknown)
Other: Females are dominant. They fight with other females in order to claim male.

AVES: DIVING BIRDS

The amazing feat of flight continues to make birds some of the most amazing animals on the planet. The entire class of birds, descended from dinosaurs, includes some of the most magnificent creatures on the planet. Since their dinosaur ancestors, birds have evolved to come in all types and shapes. Some are large birds of prey that feed on rodents; others are small fruit eaters; others sift through the ground to find bugs, and some cannot even fly. Some of the most prominent and magnificent birds are the fish-eating diving birds.

The term "diving birds" refers to the many water birds that dive for their prey, usually fish. These friends of sailors and fishermen include the kingfisher, cormorant, grebe, tern, and pelican. It is hard to go to the ocean and not see the signature outline of these magnificent birds. A bird high in the air, wings outstretched, floating on columns of air scans the water with its super-sharp eyes. In one swift movement, it pulls its wings tight to its body and slices through the air towards the water. This Olympic-class diver barely makes a splash as it enters the water and flies up again with a fish in its beak.

Nearly all of the diving birds found in the San Diego Bay eat fish. As a result, they are most commonly found near the ocean, bay, and marinas where the fisherman are unloading their catches. It has been well known for hundreds of years, that these birds are the best fishermen on the planet. While on land, the birds follow the fishermen; however, out on the ocean, it is the fishermen that follow the birds.

These animals use their keen sense of sight to see schools of fish just below the surface of the water. With the gift of flight, they soar high overhead out of sight from the fish. With their fighter jet-tuned aerodynamics, they can swoop down onto the ocean with amazing accuracy and catch up their prey. Other types of diving birds such as the common loon use a more subtle approach. They sit calmly on the surface of the water and wait for fish to calmly pass underneath them. In the blink of an eye, these peaceful looking birds can thrust themselves underwater to catch the unsuspecting fish below.

The skill and elegance of the diving birds has made them some of the most popular and well-known types of birds. Their signature dives and elegant flight denote a truly unique animal.

BELTED KINGFISHER

Ceryle alcyon

Morphology: Small with distinctive short robust bill and crown feathers. 12 to 14 in. (30-35 cm) long, blue-gray and has white beneath; the female has chestnut breast markings.
Communication: Vibrating, mechanical rattle, a scream often used as a confrontational retreat, displaying a threat, or greeting when a mate is approaching.
Range: Few nests have been found in San Diego County; they breed from Alaska across southern Canada and most of southern United Sates, during winter; Pacific Coast, north to Great Lakes and along the Atlantic Coast to New England.
Feeding: Small fish, crustaceans, reptiles, amphibians, and aquatic insects, returning to a perch to eat. Some of the fish include trout, salmon, and Atlantic salmon. They also eat mollusks, young birds, small mammals, and berries.
Locomotion: Grab most prey near surface of shallow waters. Prey is stunned when slammed against a branch; then tossed into the air, they catch it head first and swallow.
Reproduction: Dig a burrow in a bank to place their nest; often over or near water in which the birds can feed. Egg-laying occurs about from early April to early May.
Etymology: *Megaceryle alcyon* (L. *kerulos*, a sea bird; G. *alkyon*, the kingfisher)
Other: Tends to dive-bomb for prey with the sun behind: similar to strategy of fighter pilots. Were often shot by humans at fish hatcheries and by trout streams.

BRANDT CORMORANT
Phalacrocorax penicillatus

Class: *Aves* | **Order:** *Ciconiiformes* | **Family:** *Cormorant*
Morphology: The Brandt Cormorant maximum height is thirty five inches. The young of the species have a lighter breast color than the adults. It has a dark plumage and during the mating season the pouch under the bill turns cobalt blue. Its bill is hooked at the tip making it a more efficient hunter when diving for fish.
Communication: Grunts and croaks.
Range: Along the coasts of Alaska, Pacific Ocean of the US, Baja California and British Columbia.
Feeding: Main food source is fish. It hunts by swimming while using its hooked beak to catch fish. Does not always feed alone; sometimes hunts in a pack which creates the same effect as a net in the water to trap fish.
Locomotion: Flies low over the water using its powerful 49-inch wings. Wings are tapered around the edges to allow maximum efficiency. It is easily identified by its rapid wing beat and linear flight.
Reproduction: Does not have a specific location for breeding; the usual places include marshes, sea shores, or the open sea. Breeding season is during the summer in no particular place other than a rocky surface for their nest.
Etymology: *Phalacrocorax penicillatus* (L. *penicillatus* brush).

DOUBLE-CRESTED CORMORANT

Phalacrocoroax auritus

Class *Aves* | **Order** *Pelicaniformes* | **Family** *Phalacrocoracidae*
Morphology: Have large dark bodies, with a sleek, skinny head. Beaks are bright yellow and blue, small, shady, green eyes. The male are larger, and form two small tufts on their heads during mating season.
Communication: Tends to be quiet, but at times will release a small "putt." Communicates with various body gestures and movements.
Range: Inhabit most areas along the coasts of the United States and Mexico.
Feeding: Normally eat fish by diving into the water and grabbing them with their beaks.
Locomotion: Generally use their wings to get where they want to go. Sometimes will use feet to walk.
Reproduction: The males do a dance in the water. Also present the female with materials to make the nest that will house their children.
Etymology: *Phalacrocorax auritus* (L. *Phalacrocorax*, Cormorant; L. *auritus*, eared)

EARED GREBE

Podiceps nigricollis

Class: *Aves* | **Order:** *Podicipediformes* | **Family:** *Podicipedidae*
Morphology: Color changes with seasons. Both sexes look similar. Adult male has gold plumage tufts on the side of its triangular head, with bright red eyes and black crest. Neck and upperparts are black, but on the side of its body are rusty-brown or cinnamon wing feathers.
Communication: Wide variety of trills and whirrs. Frog-like cheeping notes for mating. When in danger, release single sharp chirp.
Range: Widely spread around the world. During summer, breeds located in central British Columbia, Alberta, and south-central Manitoba. In the United States, they are spread out in the northern plains and the West coast.
Winter ranges are along Pacific Coast. Thousands nest in San Diego Bay.
Feeding: Mainly aquatic insects, small fish, and their larvae. Adults feed feathers to young, with insects. Feed at the surface or dive to the bottom of a lake or bay.

Reproduction: Use ponds and marshes that have fresh to brackish water for reproduction. Breed mostly in the intermountain region and the northern parts of the Great Plains. Mating might include emerging from the water with neck extending, then swimming upright, parallel to each other.
Etymology: *Podiceps nigricollis* (L. *Podex, Podicis*-anus, L. *Pes*-foot).

PIED-BILL GREBE

Podilymbus podiceps

Class : *Aves* | **Order:** *Podicipediformes* | **Family:** *Podicipedidae*
Morphology: A small stocky brown bird. Weighs 10-18 ounces with a wingspan of 23 inches. During the summer its beak is encircled with a broad black band. Has lobed toes which are common to all grebes. Has sexual monomorphism.
Communication: Sound like "kuk-kuk-kuk, kaow, kaow, kaow, kaow, kaowk, kaowk, kawk."
Range: Live throughout America. Can be found year round in all of Central America, Western and Southern United States, and in Southern South America.
Feeding: Feeds on small fishes like sticklebacks and silversides; also aquatic insects like damselfly and dragonfly nymphs. Young grebes start by eating small insects and switch to fish as they grow.
Locomotion: They swim by paddling through the water. If they feel threatened they will dive under the water.
Reproduction: The breeding season starts in May when both sexes build the nest in 3 to 7 days. The nests are built on the water in a sheltered area. The females lay 4 to 7 elliptical eggs and take turns with the male to incubate them. The eggs hatch 23 days after they are laid.
Etymology: *Podilymbus podiceps* (L. *podicipes* - rump/foot, G. *kolymbos* - diver; L. *podicis* - rump, L. *pedis* - foot)
Other: The Pied-Billed Grebe is endangered. Reduction in wetlands has led to a decreased number of Pied-Billed Grebes throughout the Northeast.

WESTERN GREBE

Aechmophorus occidentalis

Class: *Aves* | **Order:** *Podicipediformes* | **Family:** *Podicipedidae*

Morphology: about 22-29 inches long, with a wingspan of 40 inches on average; large, long neck with a long bill of greenish yellow; small red eyes; black crown, face, and nape; dark blackish-brown back and wings; white chin, throat, and belly; feet set far back on body; female is slightly smaller than the male
Communication: A rolling "kr-r-rick, kr-r-rick!"
Range: The grebe is commonly found from Canada through California, and sometimes in Mexico. It usually occurs in the Great Plains and western states, but occasionally can be found in the eastern half of the United States. The Grebe is a migratory bird. It lives on freshwater lakes that have rushes during the breeding season. It can also be found on prairie lakes in British Columbia. Breeds from British Columbia, Saskatchewan, and Minnesota south to the Southern United States.
Food Habits: Eats fish, but also eats insects, mollusks, and crustaceans. The Western grebe is an aggressive hunter. It dives under the water and spears fish with its long bill.
Locomotion: Grebes paddle across the surface of the water with an upright posture. The Western Grebe's feet are located far back on their body which makes it difficult to walk. The ankle and toe joints are very flexible, allowing them both to paddle and steer at the same time. Dives may last 10-40 seconds. Due to the shape of their wings they need a long take off run across the water to become airborne. During migration Western Grebes fly in loose flocks but spread out to feed during the day.
Reproduction: Breeds in the spring. They have a very elaborate courtship behavior. The couple will dance and run across the water. Many grebes usually mate at the same time. The female lays three to five bluish white colored eggs. The incubation period is 20-30 days. The nest floats on the water in the reeds. Both sexes take care of the young. They become very territorial during nesting.
Etymology: *Aechmophorus occidentalis* (*Aechmophorus*: to carry a spear; *occidentalis:* Western).

CALIFORNIA LEAST TERN

Sterna antillarum browni

Class: *Aves* | **Order**: *Charadriiformes* | **Family:** *Sternidae*
Morphology: Length: 8.5 inches; wingspan: 20 inches; Diminutive tern with slender, pointed bill; very short legs; short, forked tail; smoothly rounded head without crest; pale under-wing with blurry primaries along leading edge.
Communication: Repeated kip; harsh chee-eek.
Range: Coastal waters, beaches; San Francisco Bay to San Diego.
Feeding: Small minnows and other marine or freshwater organisms.
Locomotion: Flies with very rapid wing-beats. Dives down from air for prey.
Reproduction: Nest on sandy beaches and mudflats near the ocean; aerial courtship displays; courtship feeding; usually breed at age 2 years during breeding season (May through August).
Etymology: (L. *Stern-* breastbone; L. *Antillarum* – of the Antilles; L. *Browni-* brown).
Other: ENDANGERED SPECIES; often referred to as a "gull like" bird; does not migrate.

BROWN PELICAN

Pelecanus occidentalis

Class: *Aves* | **Order**: *Pelecaniformes* | **Family**: *Pelecanidae*
Morphology: Average weight 9 lbs with a wingspan of 6 feet. Large brown bird with a long bill and pouch. Bill is 17 inches long. Has sexual monomorphism.
Communication: A snake-like hiss.
Range: Geographic distribution ranges from the Atlantic coast to the Pacific and Gulf coasts.
Feeding: Feeds on saltwater fish. Soars high above the water's surface at about 50 or 60 feet. Once it spots a fish the pelican drops from the air and plunges into the water to scoop up the fish with its pouch. This fall would kill any other type of bird, but the brown pelican is equipped with pouches of air that cushion the fall.

Locomotion: Has a wing-span of more than six feet, which helps the pelican glide. Moves its wings slowly and delicately. When in flight they glide in a U shaped formation. Plunge-dives anywhere from 10 feet to 75 feet straight into the water.
Reproduction: The male selects a nesting site to attract a female. When the female selects the male, he then starts building the nest.
Etymology: *Pelecanus Occidentalis* (L. *Pelecanus* Woodpecker; L. *occidentalis* Western.)
Other: Pelicans are a great resource for fishermen. Once a group of pelicans begins to circle and dive into the water frequently, the fisherman quickly moves to that area hoping to grab a bite.

ELEGANT TERN

Sterna elegans

Class: *Aves* | **Order**: *Charadriiformes* | **Family:** *Sternidae*
Morphology: This is a medium-large tern, with a long, slender orange bill, pale grey upperparts and white underparts. Its legs are black. In winter, the forehead becomes white. Juvenile has a scalier pale grey back.
Communication: The call is a characteristic loud grating noise like a Sandwich Tern.
Range: It breeds on the Pacific coasts of the southern US and Mexico and winters south to Peru, Ecuador and Chile. Surprisingly, this Pacific species has wandered to Western Europe as a rare vagrant on a number of occasions.
Feeding: Plunge-diving for fish, almost invariably from the sea, like most *Sterna* terns. It usually dives directly, and not from the "stepped-hover" favored by the Arctic Tern.
Locomotion: Uses wings to get around in the air, and its feet to move along on land.
Reproduction: The offering of fish by the male to the female is part of the courtship display.
Etymology: *Sterna elegans* (L. *Sterna*-to scatter; L. *elegans*- elegant)
Other: This bird is easily confused with the Royal Tern as both birds look similar; however, the Royal Tern is bigger and thicker-billed.

COMMON LOON

Gavia immer

Class: *Aves* | **Order:** *Gaviiformes* | **Family**: *Gaviidae*
Morphology: 24 inches long, wingspan 58 inches. Long body with a large bill that tapers to a point. Has red eyes with distinctive black markings.
Communication: Four identified calls. Yodel is used for territorial purposes and defense. A tremolo call is used when startled.
Range: Most abundant in Canada in Northern United States. Tend to migrate as far south as Baja California and Texas.
Feeding: Loons dive for fish after identifying them above the water visually. They eat fish and other aquatic animals including crayfish, shrimp, leeches, and some aquatic vegetation. Minnows and insects will be often eaten by the young.
Reproduction: Sexually. Breed once per year in the summer and are monogamous. Mating involves standing on the female's shoulders.
Etymology: *Gavia immer* (unknown)
Other: At special risk of lead poisoning due to preferred foods and breeding sites. They take bait from lines, taking both bait and lead sinker. Fish also poise threat of lead sinkers. Nearly 30 percent of dead loons retrieved near fresh water in Canada have been identified as being lead-poisoned.

AVES: RAPTORS

San Diego Bay, as well as San Diego County in general, is home to birds of prey known as raptors. This category of birds includes hawks, falcons, buzzards, and owls, all of which are referred to as "raptors." Because the etymology of the word raptor translates to "robber," raptors being hunters and scavengers, the name fits. Some even steal the nests and habitats of other birds because they do not feel like creating ones for themselves. The different orders of birds that belong to the bird of prey category include *Accipitroformes* (eagles, vultures, osprey, etc), *Falconiformes* (falcons), and occasionally *Strigiformes* (nocturnal birds of prey like the owl). Raptors are found worldwide, and play a very important role in ecosystems everywhere.

Raptors possess hooked beaks and sharp talons that enable them to rip open the flesh of their prey. All raptors vary in size and feather markings, but are united in the fact that they all share a common interest: pillaging, plundering, and eating whatever small creatures cross their path. They have very large wingspans and extremely powerful grips, and most can fly quite fast. They are often seen sitting broodily atop a lightpost or telephone pole, waiting patiently for their next victim.

The most commonly seen birds of prey around the Bay are the fish-hunting Osprey, the formidable Red-Shouldered Hawk, and the small Peregrine Falcon. They are solitary birds that hunt and live by themselves but can sometimes be seen being chased away from a nest or killing by more tenacious members of the *Aves* class.

OSPREY
Pandion haliaetus

Class: *Aves* | **Order:** *Falconiformes* | **Family:** *Pandionidae*
Morphology: Is 52-60cm long with a 152-167cm wingspan. It has white under parts and long, narrow wings with four "fingers", which give it a very distinctive appearance. They have reversible outer toes, and closable nostrils to keep out water during dives.
Communication: A series of sharp, annoying whistles, cheep, cheep, or yewk, yewk. Near the nest, a frenzied cheereek!
Range: Worldwide, almost cosmopolitan – mainly found by lakes, rivers, and oceans.
Feeding: Fish.
Locomotion: Flies. Osprey dive, then plunge feet first to catch their prey.
Reproduction: In March or earlier, they begin a five-month period of partnership to raise their young. Females lay 3–4 four eggs by late April, and rely on the size of their nest to help conserve heat. The eggs are the size of chicken eggs, and become fliers within eight weeks.
Etymology: *Pandion haliaetus* (Gk. *Pandion* – King of Athens exiled for over-fishing, L. *haliaetus* – eagle).
Other: Observed on top of light posts, trees, and other perches around the bay. The fish carcasses can be commonly found underneath the perch.

RED-SHOULDERED HAWK
Buteo lineatus

Class: *Aves* | **Order:** *Falconiformes* | **Family:** *Accipitridae*
Morphology: 16-24 inches long with a wingspan of 3 feet 4 inches. A hawk that looks similar to the Red-tailed Hawk, but is smaller than one, with long wings with white barring on dark wings, rusty shoulders, pale underparts barred with rust, and a narrow banded tail.
Communication: Shrill scream, kee-yeeear, with a downward inflection.
Range: Breeds from Minnesota east to New Brunswick and south to Gulf Coast and Florida, and on the Pacific Coast of California.
Feeding: Frogs, snakes, insects, and small rodents.
Locomotion: Flies with several quick wing beats and then a glide. Smoothly hovers in thermals and wind until a steep dive to catch prey.
Reproduction: Like most hawks, they build nests. The female lays 2 - 5 eggs that are incubated for 33 days. When hatched the young hawks fledge about 45 days later. In about 2 years they are sexually mature.
Etymology: *Buteo lineatus* (L. *buteo* - "a kind of hawk", L. *lineatus* - "striped").
Other: Buteo hawks are referred to as buzzards in other parts of the world. The name was mistakenly applied to vultures in North America by the early settlers.

AVES: PERCHING BIRDS

Perching birds are classified as *Passeriformes* or *passerines*, which means sparrow-shaped or songbirds. The group *Passeriformes* gets its name from the Latin name for House Sparrow (*Passer domesticus*). These types of birds consist of the largest order of the world; about 70 families are known and about 5,400 species. Thus perching birds make up 60% of all living birds; they range in many sizes from very small kinglets to the raven. They are about twice as diverse as the largest of the mammal orders (*Rodentia*). The order of *passerines* is divided in two suborders; the *Tyranni* and the *Passeri* (oscines). The oscines have more control of their syrinx (voice box) muscles which makes them true songbirds, including the crow even though they might not sound like it. The *Tyranni* (sub-oscines) are mainly tropical such as the flycatchers, ant birds, and ovenbirds. The oscines (songbirds) make up 80% of all perching bird species. Some are the sparrows, thrushes, blackbirds, and swallows.

Perching birds are medium to small land birds with feet which are adequate for perching. Most are good singers and are migratory. It is believed they are the most advanced type of birds; especially when it comes to being the most adaptive and intelligent. The most noticeable characteristic this group of birds share is the type of foot; three toes point forward and one longer toe points backwards which is adaptive to gripping a perch. If the bird begins to fall backward they have an advantage; the muscles on their tendons are designed to tighten a grip on a perch. Some of the types of perching birds include the titmouse, pipit, starling, shrike, vireo, chipping sparrow and swallow. One of the smallest perching birds is the kinglet which weighs 0.18 oz, and one of the medium-sized ones, such as the raven, weighs 3 lb. Many passerines have complex muscles which control their syrinx since many of them are songbirds; all perching birds stay in their nest as infants in wait for food from their parents. A lot of passerines are smaller than usual members of other avian orders. Some of the oscines feed on flying insects such as the swallow; others are aquatic such as the dippers which catch their prey during short dives in rivers and streams.

The origin of passerine families remained mysterious until about the end of the 20th century. Many were grouped together depending on their morphological similarity which is now believed to be the result of convergent evolution, meaning not having a close genetic relationship. The wrens from the southern hemisphere—for example, from Australia and New Zealand—look very similar and have similar behavior ways; they are very unrelated but still are put in the Passeriformes category. Today many biochemical studies are being done which are revealing a more accurate picture of passerine origins and evolution. It is thought the *passerines* evolved from Gondwana just about the time the southern super continent was breaking up leading to the *Tyranni* and after to a great radiation of forms in Australia-New Guinea where the songbirds originated from. The *Passerida* (sparrow-like forms) are believed to have originated from either the sister group or the *Crovida* (crow-like birds). They later reached the northern hemisphere where there was more explosive radiation of new species. There has been a vast amount of mixing since then because of northern forms and southern forms coming and going to the south and back again to their original habitat.

BLACK PHOEBE   *Sayornis nigricans*

Morphology: About five to seven inches long, black or sooty brown head, breast and back, white underside. Has white wing linings and outer tail feathers. Head is large and triangular. They lack wing bars. When young they are dark

gray with some brown edges to upperparts. **Range**: These birds are found in wild areas such as canyons, intermittent pools and overhanging rocks. They are a year-round resident in California, New Mexico, Arizona, west Texas and Mexico

Feeding: They eat flying insects, small fish and regurgitate pellets.

Locomotion: Usually found alone, often seen during the afternoon in search of flying insects. With an almost playful appearance it perches somewhere bobbing its tail, then swoops through the air to land on another perch close by.

Reproduction: Builds mud and grass nest, usually under something on a wall near water or farms, in towns and some natural formations in California river valleys which is their original habitat. They lay 3-6 white eggs which hatch after two weeks from being in incubation. They leave the nest very young in another two weeks after hatching; they often raise two young birds in a season.

Other: More common around fall through spring than during summer

HOUSE FINCH   *Carbonaceous mexicanus*

Class: *Aves* | **Order**: *Passeriformes* | **Family**: *Fringillidae*
Morphology: Approximately 5.5 inches tall. Males have red breast, forehead, and a stripe over the eye and rump. Adult males have rounded feathers and can range from yellow to orange-red. Immature and female are brownish and striped, although at times immature males can also have a yellowish coloration.
Range: Southern Canada and all over North America,   spreading. Habitat includes cities, suburbs, farms, canyons, feeders.
Feeding: Fruits, seeds, flowers, insect pests.
Reproduction: Breeds from March to August. In the spring males perform a courtship practice known as the "butterfly flight," whereby they ascend to 20 to 30 meters, then they slowly glide to a perch singing a loud repetitious song.
Etymology: *Carbonaceous mexicanus* (L. *Carbo-*, coal; L. *mexicanus*, pertaining to Mexico)
Other: The bright coloration comes from carotenoid pigments obtained from seeds, flowers, and fruits, which add color to their feathers during feather replacements.

ALLEN'S HUMMINGBIRD   *Selasphorus sasin*

Class: *Aves* | **Order**: *Apodiformes* | **Family**: *Trochilidae*
Morphology: Small compact bird with rusty plumage. Has a straight long black bill. Male has red throat; female has white. The body of the male is orange but the female's is green. The tails are also different; the male has an orange tail with pointed black tips while the female has orange, green, and black tail feathers with rounded white tips.
Communication: This bird does not sing. Its calls are buzzy and will also make sharp chirps.

Range: Southern Oregon to Mexican border. Southern Mexico in winter.
Feeding: They eat the nectar from flowers, small insects, and tree sap.
Locomotion: Instead of flapping wings up and down like most birds, the wings move from side to side. Wings are so fast that they have the capability to suspend in air.
Reproduction: They nest in an open cup of plant. The nest has an outer layer of grass or leaves. Can be found in shrubs or on small twigs in trees.
Etymology: *Selasphorus sasin* (L. *Selas,* Lighting or fiery meteor); *sasin,* unk.
Other: Frequent backyard feeders. One of the few early migrating North American birds.

ROCK DOVE   *Columbia livia*

Class: *Aves* | **Order:** *Columbiformes* | **Family:** *Columbidae*
Morphology: Have fat bodies, beady little eyes, and small, sharp beaks. Color consists of dark/light grey, with green and red feathers around the neck.
Communication: Use a combination of physical and vocal patterns to communicate. For casual talk, they make little "woo" noises. For mating, the males puff their bodies up and stick out their feathers to attract the females.
Range: Originated in North Africa. Slowly spread to Europe and southwest Asia. Eventually spread to the Americas and now exist worldwide.
Feeding: Are scavengers that rarely need to find their own food. Feed off of the leftovers and trash of others. If worse comes to worst, they might be forced to eat small berries instead of leftover fries.
Locomotion: To walk, the pigeons use their stubby, little feet. But to travel long distance, they use their wings.
Reproduction: Reproduce sexually. Sadly, this is done in public, and in excess.
Etymology: *Columba livia* (L. *Columba,* Dove; L. *livia,* Olive)
Other: Were once used as mailing devices. People would tie messages to their feet and set them free. Sometimes, by chance, they would find their way.

BARN SWALLOW
Hirundo rustica

Class: *Aves* | **Order:** *Passeriformes* | **Family:** *Hirundinidae*
Morphology: Small, 6 inches in length and are characterized by their dark blue head and wings and a deeply forked tail. Males and females look similar except the females' tails are a little less forked and have paler under-parts.
Communication: Barn swallow is vocal. Various methods of communication within their ability to squawk. Voice sounds like a soft "vit" or "kvik-kvik." Also "szee-szah."
Range: Can be found on every continent except Australia. Breed from Alaska to Newfoundland, Canada, and California to northern Florida in North America. Leaves breeding range in fall and travels south during the winter. Known to travel as much as 600 miles a day in large groups during migration. Also known to breed in Northern Europe, Northeastern Asia, the Middle East and North Africa. European and Asian Barn Swallows tend to travel to Southern Asia, Indonesia and Micronesia during winter migration.
Feeding: Diet consists only of insects. Grasshoppers, beetles, moths and other flying insects make up a large portion of their diet. To get water, the barn swallow flies over the surface of the water, then scoops up water in its bill.
Locomotion: Has wings which allow it to fly. Its small size requires extremely rapid and continuous wing beats with long periods of gliding.
Reproduction: Reproduces sexually. Not uncommon for barn swallows to mate in the air. When fertilized, female lays four to six eggs. Both parents help incubate the eggs and raise the young. After two weeks, the eggs hatch. Chicks will fledge after around three weeks. Same pair sometimes mates for several years.
Etymology: *Hirundo rustica* (L. *Hirundo* Swallow; L. *rustica* Country)
Other: Very versatile creature. Habitats which it lives in include farmlands, suburbs, marshes, and lake shores but are more exclusively found near man-made structures such as bridges, wharves, buildings, mine shafts, and even moving vehicles and boats. In the past barn swallows were found on rock crevices and cliff faces, but such nest sites are now rare.

MAMMALS

The characteristics of mammals evolved gradually over 200 million years ago, in a synapsid lineage. The mammalian skin is thick and protective, along with a warm covering of hair. Most mammals are also covered in hair or fur to keep them warm in cold climates. Mammals have also adapted their teeth and digestive tracts to allow various species of mammals to exploit numerous food resources. With the exception of one small group of mammals, all mammals give birth to live young (except for a select few who lay eggs instead) and nurse their young until they are able to take care of themselves.

The mammalian class is made up of thousands of species; all of these species are split up into three groups: monotremes, marsupial, and placental mammals. With the exception of arthropods, mammals are one of the most widespread class of animals around the world. One of the attributes of mammalian animals over other animals like reptiles is that mammals can maintain their body temperature regardless of outside temperatures. This allows them to survive in harsher climates, and to be more active during the day since they are not dependent on heat from the sun to get energy, and they can remain active when it gets cold.

Mammals also happen to be descended from a small group of reptiles that lived during prehistoric ages, beginning in the Triassic period. These reptiles, known as the Synapsids, were built differently from other reptiles at the time; they were built with their legs directly beneath their bodies. The creatures developed into the Therapsids during the middle of the Permiman period. Eventually, early mammals came into existence. The first mammals were small, less than ten centimeters long. There is scientific speculation that the first mammals were also nocturnal. This would explain why mammals developed endothermy, in response to the colder climate that came about at night. Many of the first mammals were predators, although there were some mammals that were herbivores and some others that were omnivorous. The first mammals also had regions of the brain that were devoted to hearing and olfactory senses, further supporting the speculation that the first mammals were nocturnal.

MARINE MAMMALS

CALIFORNIA SEA LION   *Zalophus californicus*

Class: *Mammalia* | **Order**: *Pinnipodia* | **Family**: Otariidae

Morphology: California sea lions are known for their intelligence, playful nature, and a recognizable bark. Chocolate brown is the most common color in the males, although females are often a lighter golden brown. While most males weigh around 850 pounds, some can grow to over 1,000 pounds and 7 feet long. Females are much smaller, averaging at 220 pounds, and only grow to about 6 feet in length. They have a "dog-like" face, and around five years of age males develop a bony bump on top of their skull called a sagittal crest. The top of a male's head often gets lighter with age, as is true with many human males. These members of the Otariid, or walking seal, family have external ear flaps and large flippers that they use to "walk" on land. The trained "seals" in zoos and aquaria are usually California sea lions.

Range: California sea lions are found from Vancouver Island, British Columbia, to the southern tip of Baja California in Mexico. They breed mainly on offshore islands from southern California's Channel Islands south to Mexico, although a few pups have been born on Año Nuevo and the Farallon Islands in central California.

Feeding: California sea lions are opportunistic feeders and eat such things as squid, octopus, herring, rockfish, mackerel, anchovy and whiting.

Reproduction: Most pups are born on the outer coast to the south in June or July and weigh 13-20 lbs. (6-9 kg). They nurse for at least 5-6 months and sometimes over a year. Mothers can recognize their own pups simply by sight,

the sound they make, and their smell. Pups also learn to recognize the calls of their mother. Males patrol territories and bark almost continuously during the breeding season. Gestation lasts about 50 weeks and lactation 5 to 12 months. The average lifetime of a seal is around 17 years.

Etymology: *Zalophus californianus* (L. *Zalophus* Sea Lion, L. *californianus* California).

BOTTLENOSE DOLPHIN *Tursiops truncates*

Class: *Mammalia* | **Order:** *Cetacea* | **Family:** *Delphinidiae*
Morphology: Bottlenose dolphins are grey on top, near the dorsal fin, and have a white underbelly. This makes them difficult to spot from above and below. They have an elongated upper jaw, which gave them the name "bottlenose."
Adults range between 6 and 13 feet in length, and can weigh between 330 to 1430 lbs. Dolphins living in warmer waters tend to be smaller than those in colder deeper waters. Dolphins in deeper waters also have fattier compositions, and bodies more suited for deep-sea diving. Males are slightly longer and considerably heavier than females.
Communication: Bottlenose dolphins are able to determine their surroundings through echolocation. This adaptation allows dolphins to emit high-pitched sounds, bounce them off nearby objects, and listen to the sound return to have an idea of their surroundings. Dolphins also have six air-sacs near their blowhole to produce sounds. They do not have vocal chords. Each dolphin has its own characteristic sound, which they use to identify themselves to other dolphins. Dolphins communicate extensively, but as of yet, no coherent language has been discovered.
Range: Found in all warm and temperate seas across the world. Inhabit all but the Arctic and Antarctic oceans.
Feeding: Feed mainly on small fish, and occasionally squid, crab, and similar animals.
Locomotion: Have flukes (lobes of the tail) that they move up and down to propel themselves forward. They also use pectoral fins to steer themselves in the water, and a dorsal fin for balance. Some dolphins do not have a dorsal fin and others have it placed in varying positions. Fin shapes can also vary.
Reproduction: Bottlenose dolphins have similar reproductive systems to humans. Gestation lasts 12 months, and young are usually born in shallow water. A dolphin calf is usually about three feet long at birth. Calves are usually nursed for 12 to 18 months, and stay with their mothers for up to 6 years.
Etymology: *Tursiops truncates* (L. *tursiops* front; L. *truncates* cut off, shortened -- probably refers to its nose)
Other: Bottlenose dolphins have several purposes in human culture. They are trained as performers in zoos and aquatic parks around the world. The military also uses dolphins to locate and flag mines in enemy waters. Dolphins are one of the most intelligent animals on the planet. They have well-developed brains and it is believed they are capable of feeling and emotion. Dolphin brains have a highly developed cortex, which is an indicator of their intelligence.

TERRESTRIAL MAMMALS

CALIFORNIA GROUND SQUIRREL
Spermophilus beecheyi

Class: *Mammalia* | **Order:** *Rodentia* | **Family:** *Sciuridae*
Morphology: 16-19 inches long including bushy tail weighing from 1 to 3 pounds. Grayish brown. Short ears, legs and front claws.
Communication: Consists of squeals, chirps, chirrs, whistles, and teeth clatters.
Range: From central Washington through western Oregon, California and into the northern part of Baja California.
Feeding: Squirrels eat leaves, flowers and seeds. They get most of their food from humans, their leftovers or the humans feed them.
Locomotion: Squirrels move with their four feet. Their two front feet are sometimes used as hands.
Reproduction: February through April is mating season. The babies stay underground until their eyes open.
Etymology: Spermophilus beecheyi (Gr. *sperma* seed Gr. *philos* lover, *beecheyi* after Frederick William Beechey, 1829).

DOG   *Canis lupus familiars*

Class: *Mammal* | **Order**: *Carnivora* | **Family**: *Canidae*
Morphology: All dogs are born naturally with four limbs, an abdomen, and a head. Traits are large muzzles, large canine teeth, and a long tail. The Great Dane breed may stand at 36 inches tall where the Chihuahua breed may stand at a mere 6 inches. This genetic variability has been affected by natural selection and human selection. Dogs also have incredible hearing and smelling abilities.
Communication: Dogs communicate to other dogs and humans in three ways: sound, body expression, and movement.
Range: The dog is descended from the wolf. True wolves appeared in Europe about one million years ago and in the Americas some 700,000 years later. It is probable that the dog was the first animal to be domesticated, most likely around 15,000 years ago.
Feeding: Dogs are omnivores, eating both plants and animals. Many dogs eat domestic types of food such as man-made dog food and store-bought products. However, many wild dogs eat all types of meat; chicken, beef and pork. Dogs evolved to be able to eat anything.
Locomotion: Dogs transport themselves by walking or running on all four limbs.
Reproduction: Female dogs mate only when in heat, a menstruation cycle which happens about every six months and can last anywhere between fifteen to thirty days. The size of a dog litter can vary between two to fourteen puppies, which is the largest litter a dog can have.
Etymology: *Canis lupus familiaris.* (L *Canis* dog, L. *lupus* wolf, L. *familiaris* domestic).

HUMAN   *Homo sapiens*

Class: *Mammalia* | **Order:** *Primates* | **Family:** *Hominodea*
Morphology: Erect, standing mammals that use their upper limbs to manipulate objects. Large cranial capacity for higher cognitive thought.
Communication: Humans communicate using speech. There are many different languages that humans use within their own community.
Range: Humans have the ability to adapt to any geographic region. Humans primarily live on land and can be found all over the world in even the most extreme environments.
Feeding: Humans survive by eating and drinking. Since the human body is primarily composed of water, the human body must be hydrated in order to survive. The average human can only survive about a week without water but about a month without food. Humans must eat a variety of foods to keep them healthy.
Locomotion: Humans are bipedal, meaning they walk on two legs. This allows them to walk, jog, or run, if necessary. Also, humans can walk longer distances then most animals due to the fact they are bipedal.
Reproduction: Sexual reproduction. Gestation takes place in the female's womb after the male fertilizes the egg with his sperm.
Etymology: *Homo sapien* (L. *Homo,* same; L. *sapien* man)
Other: Humans have more advanced brains then most animals. They use tools that they make to accomplish tasks with more ease. Humans are currently the only animals that walk completely upright.

BIODIVERSITY & BIOGEOGRAPHY

Geography and biology meet each other in this bio-diversity study throughout the San Diego Bay. As urban, human life continues to grow in the beautiful city of San Diego, the natural life takes a toll. This guide provides a biodiversity study that assesses the abundance and variety of intertidal life of multiple locations in the Bay. The biology of this study is combined with modern mapping technology to create biogeography. By understanding the spatial references of the study and visually comparing data to other geographic features, a new dimension of understanding is added to the study. This chapter introduces this unique marriage and explores the finer aspects of mapping and biodiversity throughout the Bay.

History of Mapping

Mapping the San Diego Bay

From its birth, map-making has been secretive. Maps have been used in wars, highly important intelligence, or traveling to locations filled with treasures and trade. Cartography, the discipline of map-making, holds many mysteries and intrigues. Although the study of cartography unravels a fascinating journey through history's mathematical and philosophical discoveries, first-hand accounts (from the individuals involved in the cartographic endeavor) are scanty. Even less common are the actual maps, charts, and original globes which were involved in the progression of cartography. The secretive nature of map-making includes stories of sea captains carrying important maps who shipwrecked their boats before allowing pirates to take maps that led to hidden treasures. Today map-making still remains secretive. As technology grows in complexity many everyday map users do not have the rudimentary skills to properly use or enjoy these. Just as in the past, many people today cannot take advantage of the wonderful world of maps. (Brown 1977)

Like many technical sciences, map-making was originally the product of curiosity. It came along as a result of the human wish to depict the environment. The first known maps came from the Babylonians, who are believed to have been making maps before 6000 B.C.E. Artifacts recovered from this ancient civilization show depictions of earth as a flat disk. Erroneous ideas about earth's shape brought fundamental questions of geometry and mathematics to ascertain the shape of the earth. (O'Connor, JJ and EF Robertson, 2005)

The first sketches (i.e. maps) made it evident to map creators, as well as users, that accuracy was essential. However, there was no scientific knowledge upon which a foundation could be established, and before going farther, one needed to be established. Hitherto, the heavy reliance primarily on the sun turned into an emphasis, eventually expanding to understanding the entirety of celestial bodies and their relationship to earth. As a result, the first milestone came when earth was proven to be a sphere. In the history of cartography, there are three prominent figures that scientifically proved the earth was spherical. (Brown 1977)

In Greece, three mathematicians and philosophers clarified the mystery of earth's shape and by doing so they helped advance the techniques of cartography. The first was Pythagoras. In 500 B.C. E., Pythagoras hypothesized that the

Earth was round after observing the height of stars and how ships appeared on the horizon. He noticed that the top of the masts appear first, then the sails and finally the hulls. The second most influential Greek, Aristotle, in 300 B.C. E., noticed lunar eclipses. He logically deducted that the earth must be a sphere since it casts a rounded shadow on the moon. Lastly, in about 150 A.D., Ptolemy, a mathematician, geographer and astronomer, created an eight-volume work called *Geographia* that showed many maps of the world. Ptolemy was the first to implement lines of latitude on maps. These are imaginary lines that helped describe the location of a point on Earth. The lines start at the Equator at 0° and go to up to the North Pole (90° N) and down the South Pole (90° S). (Brown 1977)

During the Middle Ages the work of Ptolemy was lost; subsequently the progress of cartography stopped as Europe fell into the Dark Ages. Ptolemy's work was not accurate—his measurement of earth's circumference was too small—nevertheless, Ptolemy had the right concepts. His geographic speculation was the key to unlocking the next step in the puzzle. During the Middle Ages, maps became largely decorative, even religious symbols, and most cartographers started depicting Jerusalem as the center of the world. The influence of the church was oppressive. For about twelve hundred years it was considered sinful to probe the mysteries of the universe and the explanations set forth by the church regarding earth and the heavens were not to be questioned. Maps were produced under the church and to a large degree these were awe-inspiring, yet vague enough to quench the curiosity of the common observer. To defy the church could result in severe consequences, and as a result, only heretics and those brave enough to bear these consequences proceeded with their geographic speculation. (O'Connor, JJ and EF Robertson 2005)

As Europe awoke from the Dark Ages, math and science flourished, and with this a revived interest in cartography led to the next stepping-stone in being able to produce an accurate map of earth. Countries (especially Spain and Portugal) were heavily investing in expeditions to the New World, and logically they wanted a return on their investments. Navigation was the key. Unfortunately, navigation was difficult because at the time there was no system to tell location at sea; so of those that ventured to sea many never came back. With plane coordinate geometry, accredited to Renee Descartes, in the 1600's, earth's geometry system gradually came into realization. (Brown 1977)

With Descartes, development of plane coordinate geometry, an abstract frame of reference for flat surfaces was created. Any point's position could be indicated with regards to the horizontal (x) axis and the vertical (y) axis. In this manner, the position of any point could easily be plotted in the Cartesian plane and the position of any point relative to another could be shown. After cartographers and geographers established the spherical nature of earth, concepts from the Cartesian coordinate geometry quickly became useful. It was incorporated into earth's geometry system; nonetheless the challenge proved greater with the geometry of a sphere. (O'Connor, JJ and EF Robertson 2005)

Map-Making in San Diego Bay

The complexity of cartography stretches beyond just map prints; it incorporates three fields, all of which are equally important in the final product. These three components of map-making are the techniques and tools used to survey, the medium of print, and the style of the map. A shortcoming in any field leads to a distortion in the final print. (Brown 1977)

Changes in instruments and techniques through time have been evident. In mapping San Diego, there were various changes in map technology. It is important to note that while the mapping of San Diego Bay was done with reasonable frequency, there was a lag in technology when compared to the modes that were being employed in the East Coast and Europe. (Strickland 2005)

Since the Spanish first arrived in the Port of San Diego, a rich history of San Diego Bay mapping has accumulated. Despite the loss of a few maps here and there, the history of San Diego Bay is well kept. Cabrillo, the first European visitor to San Diego in 1542, left no evidence of maps from his expedition to the port.

Sixty-two years after Cabrillo, the first extant map of San Diego Bay dates from Vizcaino's expedition in 1602. This map is a rough sketch, understood to be synonymous with San Diego Bay at the time. The techniques employed here use minimal scientific knowledge or technology. (If there were any instruments used, perhaps the artist used an astrolabe to estimate angles he did not take the time to survey in the field.) The sketch does not include latitude and longitude and there is no evidence any attempt was made. The directions north and south are probably based upon wind direction. (Strickland 2005)

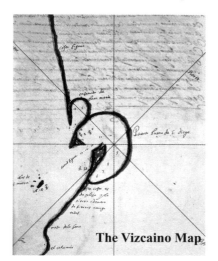

The Vizcaino Map

The next map of San Diego Bay which demonstrates a change in technique is known as the Pantoja Map. In 1782, Juan Pantoja mapped the San Diego Bay and its surroundings, giving history its first detailed map of the area. In a seven-week field survey, Pantoja, a cartographer and geographer on his way to Monterrey Bay, made a refined version of what is still considered a sketch. One can speculate that Pantoja used more sophisticated tools such as an astrolabe to measure angles and basic techniques of triangulation. By 1789 derivatives of the Pantoja map appeared in England and France. (Harlow 1987)

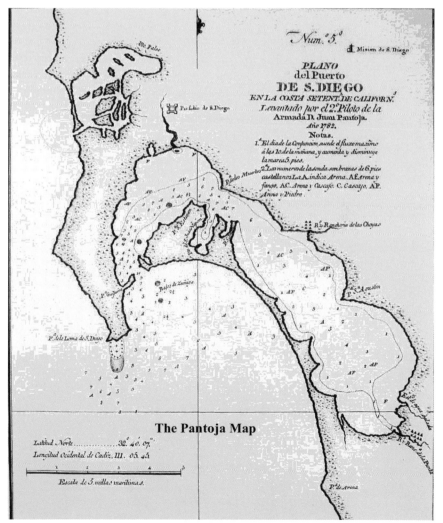

The Pantoja Map

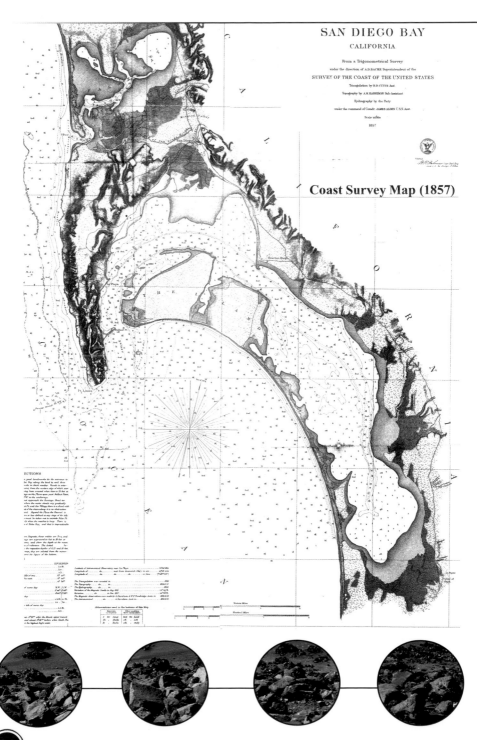

SAN DIEGO BAY

CALIFORNIA

From a Trigonometrical Survey

under the direction of A.D.BACHE Superintendent of the

SURVEY OF THE COAST OF THE UNITED STATES

Triangulation by R.D.CUTTS Asst.

Topography by A.M.HARRISON Sub-Assistant

Hydrography by the Party

under the command of Comdr. JAMES ALDEN U.S.N. Asst.

Scale 1:20000

1857

Coast Survey Map (1857)

The Pantoja map remained the quasi-official map of San Diego till 1848. With the Treaty of Guadalupe Hidalgo, settling Mexican-American territory disputes, San Diego officially became American territory and new maps were drawn of San Diego. Thus in 1857, with San Diego Bay now a part of the United States, state of the art maps were needed. Using triangulation and new map printing techniques, the U.S. Coast Survey mapped San Diego Bay. The map was used for navigational purposes and includes details such as linear scales in statute and nautical miles. There are latitude and longitude figures in the margins. At lower left, sailing direction and notes on courses and bearings, soundings, and tides are included. (Harlow 1987)

By the late 1880's mapping techniques and surveying methods had changed. US Geodetic Surveys (USGS) were now being conducted. A geodetic survey is one in which ellipsoidal earth figures are used (exact latitude and longitude lines compensating for flattening at the poles). In 1902, the US Geodetic Survey (USGS) published a complete map of San Diego. Whereas in the past maps focused primarily in the Bay, this map covered the entirety of the city. This USGS Topographic Map Series is based on interlocking latitude and longitude grids. The grid quadrangles in such maps are not themselves complete wholes, but together form a single map. Each grid, however, allows for individual handleable size map sheets, and each grid square can individually be revised. (Strickland 2005)

The next map of San Diego Bay that demonstrates a change in technique dates to 1967. To create this map a method known as photogrammetry was used. Photogrammetry is an aerial remote sensing technique, the latest innovation at the time. In photogrammetry, a high-resolution aerial camera uses global satellite navigation technology to place a camera over the designated photo block. In 1967, the technique was not as advanced as it is today. However, photogrammetry did allow for some advances. To this day, most maps are created using photogrammetric methods. (US Geodetic Map 1967)

One other advance made at this time was cartographers' ability to apply accurate scales to their maps. By using scaled photographs, cartographers could then transfer this scaled information directly to their maps. ("DART" 2005)

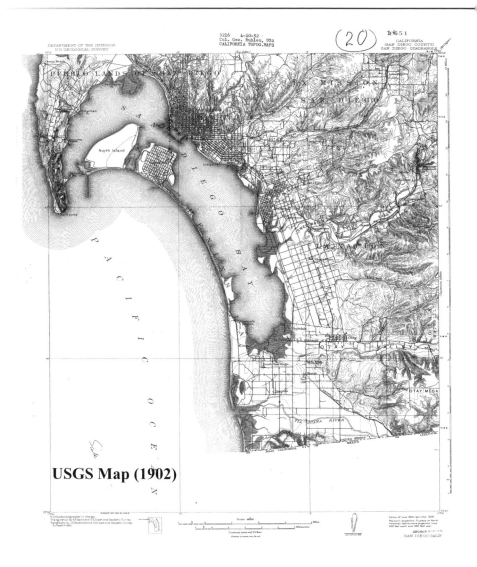

DEPARTMENT OF THE INTERIOR
U.S GEOLOGICAL SURVEY

3216   4-10-52
Col. Geo. Ruhlen, USA
CALIFORNIA TOPOG. MAPS

(20)

1 6 5 1

CALIFORNIA
(SAN DIEGO COUNTY)
SAN DIEGO QUADRANGLE

USGS Map (1902)

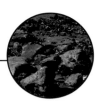

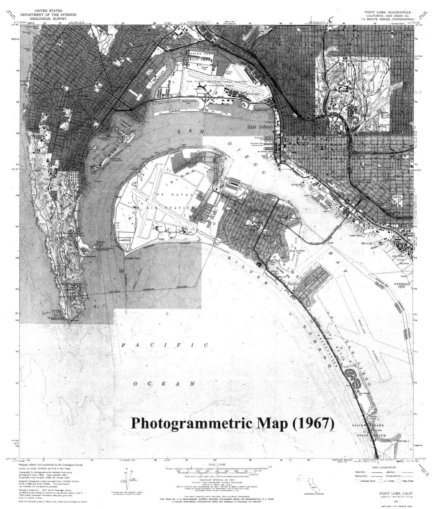

Photogrammetric Map (1967)

The Future of Cartography: Geographic Information Systems

Until the arrival of Geographic Information Systems (GIS), maps were generally done to depict location for navigational purposes. With GIS Technology, all of that was to change. Cartography moved beyond the general to the thematic. Now maps and other GIS depiction could provide information beyond that found in classic maps.

Unlike ancient methods of navigation, which were done with such tools as a sextant, today, satellites and radio signals are the primary source for recording location via global positioning systems. Geographic information systems are computer application tools used to store, analyze and display data that have a spatial component in order to aid in visualization and decision-making. Not only does GIS give us the location, it also employs software that allow us to see statistically

both quantity and quality of desired components. (Howser 2005)

It is estimated that 80% of all data have some kind of spatial configuration. For example, data from a list of addresses, or a series of Caribbean plantations, or even the locations of a particular invertebrate can be located and configured in a map complete with representation of their quantity and qualities. Today we have questions such as, where should the City of San Diego assign more police officers with a limited labor pool and budget? This decision is made easier by mapping the types of crime, the times that they occur, and the number of incidents on a GIS map. Where is the next earthquake likely to occur? By using GIS map layers of historical earthquakes, faults, seismic plate boundaries, scientist can conduct risk analysis. The potential of GIS spans to all disciplines and application is not only incredible, but tremendously useful.

Obtaining data is the costliest and most time-consuming process of creating a GIS map. There are many pre-made datasets from groups and organizations such as the US Geological Survey and various governmental entities such as the City of San Diego. Most GIS users use existing datasets and convert them to a format that GIS can manipulate and depict. However, when new and important questions are asked, many times new and uncollected data is required. During the course of the completion of the Field Guide we have attempted to collect new data regarding the distribution of intertidal species in SD Bay. Collecting new GIS data is very costly and time-consuming. We have nevertheless found the effort worthwhile, as we hope the Field Guide will demonstrate.

Conclusion

As discussed in this paper, in the past, maps were held in secret for the sheer power of their important information. The very techniques of mapmakers were held in check by the power of the state. In addition, the scientific, mathematical, and philosophical approaches were not always correct. At times, hundreds of years elapsed before the combined efforts of many resulted in a scientific or mathematical advance. Cartography, despite the odds against it, has nevertheless progressed through the centuries. Today, the world of maps is not so secretive, but it does remain somewhat inaccessible. The complexity of the technologies which it employs, and the complexity of the science and math (GIS techniques included), puts maps, at times, beyond the general public understanding. With the arrival of the internet, the popular Google search engine and Mapquest, to name a few, maps and their widespread use may be coming out of their hiding places to be enjoyed by all. (Brown 1977)

Sources:

Brown, Lloyd A. The Story of Maps. New York: Dover Publications, Inc., 1977.

Harlow, Neal. Maps of the Pueblo Lands of San Diego 1602-1874. Los Angeles: Dawson's Book Shop, 1987.

Howser, Tony. "A Scalable Skill Certification Program in GIS." Email Interview San Diego State University, San Diego Mesa College, SD City Schools, and National Science Foundation Grant. 2005.

NCGIA Core Curriculum in GIS Science. Comp. Kirvan, Anthony P, et all.1997. *Department of Geography, University of Texas at Austin*, USA. 27 May 2005 <www.ncgia.ucsb.edu/education/ curricula/giscc/units/u014/u014. html>.

O'Connor, J J., and E F. Robertson. Longitude and the Académie Royale. Feb. 1997. 27 May 2005 <http://www-groups.dcs.st-and.ac.uk/~history/Hist Topics/Longitude1.html>.

Photogrammetry Explained. 2005. DARTmap.com. 27 May 2005 <http://www. dartmap.com/faq_-_photogrammetry.htm>.

Strickland, Muriel. Introduction. Mapping San Diego County: An Introduction to the Holdings of the SDHS Archives Map Collection. San Diego: San Diego Historical Society. 2005.

Strickland, Muriel. Personal interview. 25 May 2005.

Mapping Technique Comparison

As technology has advanced, so has the ability to accurately record spatial data on maps. Below are a few examples comparing multiple techniques of mapping the same area. All of these maps are representations of the Boat Channel, an extension of the San Diego Bay.

The following is a diagram that was drawn while standing on the shore using visual cues to create a representation of what the artist thought the Boat Channel looked like from above. Obvious landmarks are represented on the map with only an approximation of distance and proportion. This technique is an example of some of the most primitive forms of surveying.

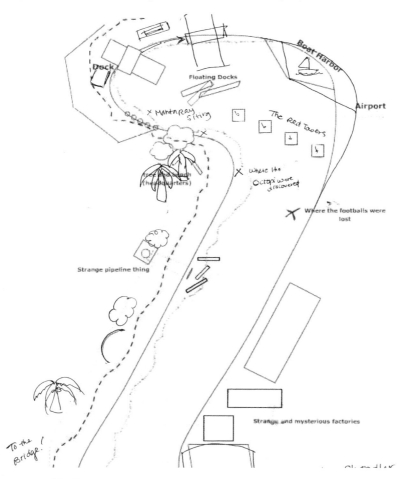

This next map compares the difference between eyesight and precise placement with Global Positioning System (GPS) technology. The black lines are another artist's rendering of what he believes the end of the boat channel looks like. The red lines were created using GPS surveying. In order to generate the red line, a survey team recorded their latitude and longitude every few yards using the Garmin Etrex® GPS system. Once enough data points had been collected, the points were plotted and then a line was traced through them. This method allows for accuracy, limited only by the accuracy of the GPS signals.

The overlay demonstrates how general shapes and outlines are similar, but only the GPS method allows for precise orientation, distance, and proportion.

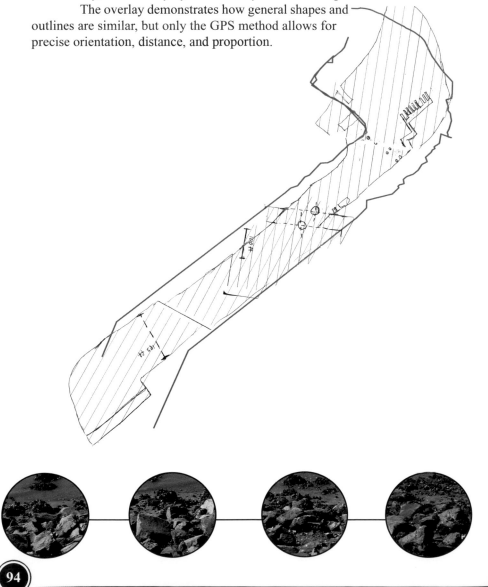

With high-resolution aerial and satellite photography, the next comparison can be seen. This image is high-resolution aerial photography with the GPS generated survey lines overlaid on top of it. The accuracy of the image is only limited to the resolution of the pixels. In this case, each pixel is approximately 12 inches in the real world. The GPS line (the white line on the image) which looked so accurate in the previous image has many places where the line appears jagged and not on the proper path. When the GPS survey points were collected, the survey team attempted to follow the coastline exactly. The error in the plotted GPS line represents the amount of error in standard, commercially available GPS systems, which can be anywhere between 15 to 30 feet.

Introduction

One of the main aspects of this guide was a study in species abundance and diversity across northern San Diego Bay, from the Coronado Bridge to the mouth of the Bay. As humans and nature continue to clash, as artificial replaces natural, this guide provides insight into the spectrum of intertidal creatures that have survived throughout the Bay. In order to assess the living creatures, various sites were surveyed across the coastline of the Bay. Harbors, inlets, channels, and beaches were a few of the places that the survey teams looked through in their search for life.

Sections of shoreline were laid with transects to observe, quantify, and classify the creatures at certain tide heights. The goal of this study was not only to compare life across the bay, but also to describe the changes in habitats at different tide heights of the intertidal zones. Once the creatures had been counted and archived, geography and cartography was needed to display and make sense of the vast amounts of data that had been collected over a three-month period.

It was predicted that the species abundance and diversity would differ by location due to several factors. The causative variables may include the distance from the ocean (mouth of the bay, enclosed harbor compared with open channel), and the differences in human activity at the site.

The biodiversity study of this field guide called for a need to accurately plot species distribution across the bay using our own form of biogeography. In order to give this data spatial meaning, Geographic Information Systems (GIS) were used to place the data throughout San Diego. Satellite photography, coastal surveys, and GPS data collected by the survey teams were combined to generate maps showing species distribution throughout the bay. With the help of modern GPS technology, the survey teams were able to place the data extremely accurately.

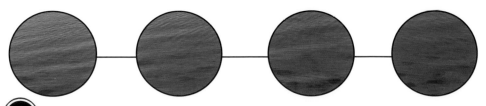

Methods of Data Collection

To quantify the species at a given location, we had to have a system by which we would measure them. The first step was to create a grid by which we could count and quantify the creatures within the grid. A 0.5 meter by 0.5 meter square frame made of PVC pipe made the outline of our grid. Due to the sheer size of a 0.25 meter^2 square, only the corners of the 0.25 meter^2 plot were used. By stringing line across our plot, four 10 cm by 10 cm square, were made at each of the four corners of the 0.25 meter^2 plot.

The next step was to know where to place the plot in order to count the creatures at the different tidal heights along the beach. To begin, a tide chart from SIO was used to find the exact time at which the low and high tide would be at a 0 foot tide height. A pole was then placed in the ground to mark the 0 foot spot. Once we knew where the 0 foot mark was, five ropes were laid perpendicular to the water line approximately 2 meters apart from each other to create transect lines on the shore. Along each transect line at the 0 foot tide mark a plot was placed on the ground.

Next was to observe the creatures underneath each plot. Only the 10 cm by 10 cm squares at the 4 corners of the plots were used to observe what was inside them. For each of the 10 cm by 10 cm squares, the composition of the ground (rock or sand), and the type and number of a particular species were recorded. Once each of the four corners had been recorded, the plot was moved.

To address the intertidal zonation at each site we used a novel method to precisely find the location of the -1', 0', +1', +2', +3', and +4' tide heights. From the marker pole that was placed at the 0' tide height, one foot was measured up from the bottom of the pole. At that point, a laser attached to a bubble level was leveled and then shot until it hit somewhere on the transect line +1 up the slope from the previous survey mark. The point where the leveled laser hit the

transect line was the +1 foot tide height location.

The plots were then moved up the transect line and everything was surveyed once again at the +1 foot tide height mark. This method alleviated the necessity to wait for the tides to come in and out. The process was repeated until all of the tide heights along the transect line were surveyed (from -1' or 0' to +5'). Once this happened, the transect line was picked up and in a leap-frog fashion was placed another 2 meters down the beach.

When the transect line was placed down again, all of the steps repeated until a substantial portion of a particular beach had been surveyed. Each site included 15 to 30 transects.

While the survey data of the living

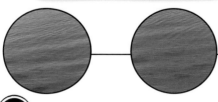

creatures was being collected, the geographic portion of the survey had to also be created. For each of the sites that were surveyed, GPS units were used to mark the boundaries of a particular survey site. These were obtained by collecting the GPS coordinates for each of the corners of the area being surveyed and then plotting out the area on a computer.

Once we had a polygonal plot of the survey area, the location could be then geo-referenced to satellite imagery and other survey plots to generate the maps that showed the distribution of species across San Diego Bay.

There was one instance in which we had access to a system called a differential GPS. While normal GPS units have an accuracy of approximately 20 feet, a differential GPS has accuracy to within 8 inches. After collecting data and using algorithms that correct for atmospheric interference, extremely accurate survey results can be collected. At the Coronado survey locations, we were able to use this system to map out the locations of the individual plots; a feat nearly impossible with normal GPS units.

Intertidal Zonation

Zonation is the sub-classification of biomes into smaller zones that share unique physical characteristics. Each provides a unique habitat that favors various species that exist in these zones. Intertidal zones are identified by the horizontal bands that are made up on the shore. The tide rises and ebbs which causes some areas to receive more water in any given tide cycle. This results in a different habitat for every tidal height. Particular species are usually more adapted to a certain range on the shore of which they can receive their ideal amount of water. This results in segregation of species into zones on the shore.

The supralittoral zone is the area almost permanently exposed to air except for high tides and high waves. It is the most likely to be destroyed by human interference. The range is approximately 7 feet to its lower limits to approximately 2.5 feet below mean sea level. Usually barnacles are the most likely to live in this area, but in small amounts.

The midlittoral zone is covered and uncovered twice a day by the tides.

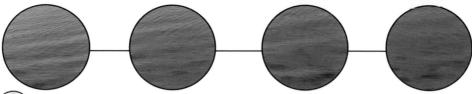

Usually the animals in this area are adapted to being completely immersed in water. For example, sea anemones close when the tide is out in order to keep in the moisture which is necessary for their survival. It is usually from 2.5 feet to 0 feet. Acorn barnacles, mussels, goose neck barnacles, crabs, periwinkles, chitons, snails, limpets, sea anemone and whelks are not uncommon in this area.

The infralittoral zone is the lowest part of the shore exposed only to the lowest tides. Most organisms from the intertidal zone call this area home. The algae and surf grass provide shelter for many small animals and provide plentiful food in this zone. This is from approximately -0.1' to -1.8'. This can be referred to as the "sublittoral zone." Animals that live here cannot tolerate complete submersion and thrive by the constant action of the motion of the ocean.

For animals that can survive and thrive in the intertidal zone, this is a harsh and challenging place to live. However, it can be an area rich with nutrients and one that provides an abundant supply of both oxygen and water.

Infralittoral
-2' to 0'

Midlittoral
0' to 1'

Supralittoral
0' to 4'

Tides

The casual visitor and marine biologist like must take into account the tides when visiting the intertidal zone. The earth, moon, and sun are the three controlling elements involved in oceanic tides. The force that occurs between these bodies is gravitational attraction. Depending on the different alignments and geographic location one might see an assortment of high and low tides. These tides can become predictable and exhibit periodic cycles. The moon is the controlling factor in this cycle that lasts 24 hours and 50 minutes, and the time between high and low tides usually lasts six hours and thirteen minutes. As a result, at any given time there will always be two high and low tides on earth. This gravitational pull exerts more force on the part of earth nearest to it. Such an event results in the bulging of the ocean since the ocean is more liquid than the rigid crust of the earth. They both undergo bending and warping; however the ocean is more flexible and so gravity's pull is more evident. Oddly enough, this appears true even when earth's floating plates are higher above the ocean and thus are pulled with greater force.

      The extent of gravitational pull done by both the sun and moon is determined by their mass and distance from earth. The moon is approximately 240,000 miles from earth, whereas the sun is 93 million miles away. For this reason the moon exerts 2.2 times the gravitational pull as the sun does. Even though the moon is closer it only contributes to 56% of earth's tidal energy, while the sun does 44%. The sun exerts this much force even though it is much farther because it has a greater mass than the moon, the moon's mass being 7.35×10^{22} kg and the sun's being 1.98×10^{30} kg. The speed of tides can reach up to 5 m/second and will mix the content of the coastal water, having been known to impede ship navigation. Tides rise and fall at a steady rate and can rise on an average of three feet in eight to twelve hours. The tide ranges in different geographic land regions. For example, in the Bay of Fundy, the tide can rise to a record forty feet in six hours.

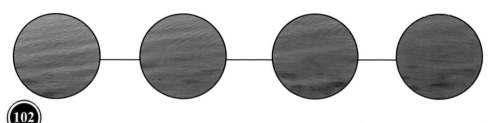

San Diego Bay has a maximum tidal swing of 9.5 feet. The rising tide is called a flood and lowering is called an ebb. Another influence is the varying distance between the sun, moon, and earth. Since the earth and moon do not travel in a circle but rather an ellipse they exhibit a higher degree of pull as they are on a nearer path.

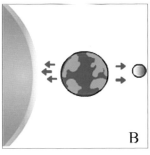

A

High tide occurs in two ways, the first being when the moon and sun are aligned, and together their gravitational pull act on the ocean. This is called a new moon. Known as a spring tide, this occurs twice a month and pertains to the largest difference between high and low tides.

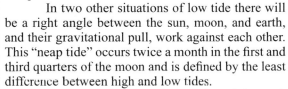

B

The other is when the earth is in between the sun and moon and there is a less high tide called a full moon. This is not the highest tide because the gravitational attraction of the sun and moon do not complement each other.

In two other situations of low tide there will be a right angle between the sun, moon, and earth, and their gravitational pull, work against each other. This "neap tide" occurs twice a month in the first and third quarters of the moon and is defined by the least difference between high and low tides.

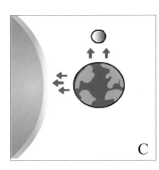

C

Even with the given knowledge of the earth and moon's pathways, tidal predictions are not entirely accurate based on just these influences. One must also consider more in tune coastal factors such as the shape of the coast, depth contours off shore, local water currents, and other factors such as water salinity and nearby estuary water flow. This explanation has long been accepted but is now being brought under scrutiny. Many insist on a different explanation for the behavior of tides. One theory is that as the moon passes directly overhead a land mass, it will pull the land higher than the ocean, resulting in the draining of the sea.

Diagram A: Spring Tide, new moon.
Diagram B: Full Moon
Diagram C: Neap Tides, quarter moon.

PLACES AND SPACES

OF THE SAN DIEGO BAY

INTEGRATING BIOLOGY AND HUMANITY THROUGHOUT THE BAY

This section of the guide is designed to familiarize readers with a variety of locations scattered throughout San Diego Bay. Each location features a wealth of pictures and information that includes a history of the site as well as a description of its current uses to the San Diego community. Also interspersed throughout the chapter are nature reflections and poems that were inspired by the many facets of the Bay. By using geographic information systems (GIS), a section is also devoted to portraying the location and the biodiversity of the site. This chapter will give the reader a better understanding of a few of the many interesting places and spaces around San Diego Bay.

BOAT CHANNEL

History of the Boat Channel

The Boat Channel's existence has produced many controversies over the years. Currently, there is a conflict over who holds responsibility for its clean-up between the City of San Diego and the Navy. The Navy once used the area known as the Naval Training Center (NTC), which included the Boat Channel as a training facility. Recently, however, the Navy transferred the ownership to the city as part of the Clinton-era military closings. The city's new redevelopment project for NTC called for a public park along the Boat Channel's shoreline. However, the city does not want the financial liability for the Boat Channel's clean up due to the cost. ("Boat Channel | Naval Training Center" 2005)

The Boat Channel contains sediment with high levels of lead, copper, zinc, and DDT, which is a banned pesticide. Navy records show that there are

Hundreds of years ago, the San Diego River used to flow though this small inlet as it dumped into the Pacific. You would never guess that by its modern appearance. Its location between the international airport, the old Naval Training Center, and a former dumpsite has turned this dredged and artificial channel into what it is today. Yet there is still life clinging to the rocks and in the shadows of the intertidal zones. Even in the heart of human civilization, natural life still exists.

around fifty to sixty areas of the NTC that have been poisoned. Though this amount of toxins is normal for large military bases, it is not normal for the residents or public parks within a city's limits. (McNab 2005) (Fact Sheet NO. 5 1996)

The Boat Channel was labeled a polluted area by the city. The air quality in the Boat Channel area also has come into question by the city. The end of the Boat Channel has released benzene and vinyl chloride hundreds of times the legal limit into the air. The soil around the Boat Channel also came into question when a recent discovery of a large toxic burn dump near the grounds of High Tech High school was discovered. Sites within NTC were used as late as the seventies for burning garbage disposal. After these landfill sites served their purpose, they were capped with soil, trapping in the toxins left behind. These toxins included infectious wastes, paint wastes and thinners, and carcinogenic metals. Although

the military base was blamed for this, there have been no measures to clean up the environmental hazards. (McNab 2005) (Fact Sheet NO. 5 1996)

On March 18, 2004, the San Diego City Manager's Office finally took action by recommending that the City take steps to de-pollute the Boat Channel at NTC. Jim Madaffer, a chairman of the Council's Natural Resources and Culture Committee, told City staff members to conduct more detailed research in order to make another proposal to the City about the Boat Channel. What may happen remains to be seen. The responsibility for carrying out the clean up is debated between the Navy and the City. No one wants to take the

responsibility. It seems as though development will be at a halt until someone picks up the bill for the cleaning of the Boat Channel. (Powell 2004)

Uses

When traveling to sunny Southern California, there is no better place to bring the family than the majestic decaying shores of the San Diego Boat Channel. Located directly underneath the eternally operating Lindberg airfield's flight path, it is sometimes a calm and tranquil piece of nature to enjoy. Once used as a draining point for the runoff and a training site for a bustling Navy Training Center, it is now a disease-ridden body of water.

Do not let its putrid smell fool you. There are dozens of things for the whole family to enjoy. You and the kids can take a swim to the floating docks, but be sure to have your tetanus and hepatitis shots. While enjoying a wonderful nature hike along a forgotten trail, do watch out for broken glass and barbed wire. Better yet, integrate the family's sunbathing activities on the broken slabs of sharp concrete walls of the Boat Channel with the identification of different vermin that live along and among those slabs. Whatever you choose to do, we urge you to take a day to visit San Diego's most valued natural treasure—the Boat Channel.

Location

The San Diego Boat Channel is located near the old Naval Training Center (NTC), just off Rosecrans Street. It extends northward from the San Diego Bay and jut away from the Bay's waters at the Spanish Landing. To the west of the Channel is the massive redevelopment of Liberty Station and to the east is Camp Nimitz and the San Diego International Airport. The Boat Channel was created from marshlands. In 1922, when the soil was dredged from the Boat Channel marshland, the Navy reclaimed

the material to build the NTC. In 1923, NTC construction began on 135 acres of highland and 142 acres of tideland, donated by the City of San Diego and San Diego Chamber of Commerce to the Navy.

During the construction period, the shoreline of the San Diego Bay extended further inland than it is currently. The area near the Spanish Landing at the North Athletic Area and Camp Farragut was entirely underwater. In 1939, a construction plan was authorized to make further improvements of the Boat Channel, which was to be deepened, and 130 acres of filled land were added to the eastern boundaries of the NTC. Today, the average depth of the Boat Channel is 12-15 feet. The deepest is 27 feet at its lowest point. When dredging ended, the Boat Channel had become a carved out "L" shaped from the marshlands. Though construction for the Boat Channel is completed, development around it continues to this day.

Description and Feeling

To get to the Boat Channel, we had to hike through the old section of the Naval Training Center. As we looked around, a sense of desolation and abandonment came over us. Seeing all the broken glass and empty buildings almost made us want to turn back. But the end was near and water was in sight.

The sense of security was soon destroyed, when we stumbled past an old broken-down pier. After seeing the pier and the old beaten seats along the trail, our hopes for a pleasant beach experience were lost. As energy drained out of our systems, complaints began to rise in everyone's mind. Thoughts of how uneventful and dreadful the day was going to be ran through our minds.

Knowing that first impressions are not always right, we tried to make the best of our situation. One of us even took a swim and came out happy, though he smelled like sewage. We were able to see creatures that some of us have only seen on the Discovery Channel, such as shorebirds, octopi, crabs, and all sorts of invertebrates. With the day coming to an end, we realized that a beach does not need white sand to be considered beautiful. If there was ever a place to break the norm and release the inner child, it was the Boat Channel.

Sources

Boat Channel | Naval Training Center. The City of San Diego. 19 May 2005.
<http://www.sandiego.gov/ntc/amenities/boatchannel.shtml>.
Fact Sheet No. 5. Naval Training Center BRAC Environmental Coordinator. 19 May 2005.
<http://www.efdsw.navfac.navy.mil/Environmental/pdf/ntcfs5.pdf>.
McNab, John. "Save Our NTC." Save Our NTC, Inc., San Diego CA. 19 May 2005. <http://www.ntcsd.org/about.html>.
Powell, Ronald W. "Much of NTC has Changed in Past Years." Union-Tribune. 5 Dec. 2004.
<http://www.signonsandiego.com/uniontrib/20041205/news_1m5ntcnext.html>.

The Empty Channel
A Nature Reflection

Above the water's surface, the Boat Channel is a desolate place. Slime, mussels, and the occasional predatory bird mark the shoreline. Factory drain pipes, the airport, buildings and construction sites all spill across the water. The wake of a boat occasionally breaks against the shore, disturbing the dull silence. I enjoy the break in the monotony for a moment, until the sky splits in half from the sound of the jet turbines screaming overhead. I can't stay up here any longer; I'm dying to dunk my head below the surface of the water to chat with the fishes. For now, I must find contentment sitting here in the hot sun, breathing the dry air and the jet fumes.

       —Merlin Gunn-Cicero

Potential
A Nature Reflection

Taking in this whole place, I have seen a Mecca of human exploration and recreation. I haven't seen much natural life by the shore. Maybe the shore isn't where I should be looking. I don't know what dwells beneath the water's surface. In the hour that I have been here, I have seen boat traffic; but my vision has been confined to this narrow Boat Channel. All that traffic will spread out when the Channel opens into the Bay, and the bay opens into the Pacific Ocean. I see potential focused in one spot, and all those boats are ready to carry that potential.

       —Merlin Gunn-Cicero

Broken Links

Transform, transcribe, and translate
The antiparallel polar chains of humanity's makeup turn actions into reactions
The spectrum of my truth serum
Bumps upon my scandal
I cast my feet and hands into the sea
Let my head lie by the dry sand
Wither away wither away
I have barely made a scratch
"will I be remembered?" echoes in the far distant
From where my reality came, I care not about remembrance
Living on
Wither away, wither away

—Khoa Tran

The Boat Channel

Boat Channel, currents flowing,
Lights on water, shining, glowing.
Boats wait anxiously at the channel's docks,
Rocking, floating, bells ringing with the clocks.
Their decks are dry and warm, their hulls are pearly white,
Sea salt hangs in the air,
Oh, the Boat Channel, what a sight.

People come and people go, laughing and talking,
Do they wished they owned a priceless piece?
In quiet ripples, the water breaks against the silent sea walls.
Shore rocks standing like a mighty fortress.
The heron hunts and the seagull gives its call.
Boat channel, currents flowing,
Lights on water, shining, glowing.

—Ben Lewis

Biology of The Boat Channel

Octopus Garden

The average octopus is said to be extremely intelligent; they choose their own habitats to keep themselves away from predators. Why are there so many octopi at the San Diego Boat Channel? An octopus can choose its own habitat to live in. You can see abundant octopi habitats at the Boat Channel. Since the Boat Channel is filled with plenty of harmful chemicals and sewage drains, it is unlikely for this place to be a tourist spot for visitors that happen to stroll along. Therefore, few humans are around to disturb or fish this amazing creature.

Octopi reside in rocky areas throughout the Boat Channel shoreline. They establish dens in rocky areas or caves, and smaller individuals may dig dens in sand-shell substrates. The Boat Channel is filled with many octopus dens which are mainly located on the shore of the bay and sand. The reason for this is because they are camouflaged, which allows them to hide from predators. The octopus' predators include seals, sea lions, sea otters, dogfish, lingcod, flatfish and larger octopi. These predators are not located around the Boat Channel, allowing the octopi to thrive. An octopus can escape from its predators by shooting a jet of water through its body to create a burst of speed.

Under water, they can crawl along the bottom of the sea floor by using their tentacles as legs as they slither through crevices under rocks. There are many rocky areas in the Boat Channel where the octopus dens can be easily seen. An oc-

topus den mainly looks like a hole surrounded by a ring of rocks 3-4" in diameter. An octopus lives in this habitat to keep away from predators. The Boat Channel is a safe haven for octopi to live because it is a sheltered place with very few visitors that stroll by.

Interactions of The Boat Channel

San Diego Wetlands

Wetlands are transitional lands between terrestrial and aquatic systems where the water table is usually at or near the surface or the land is often covered by shallow water during some parts of the year. Wetlands can be categorized according to specific habitat and type of vegetation. Saltwater and brackish water marshes, which are usually located in coastal areas, are located in wetlands. Also, there are freshwater wetlands, which are primarily in the inland areas of California, and then there's the freshwater forested and scrub wetlands, which are commonly referred to as riparian habitat.

The South San Diego Bay Unit was the dream of San Diego's environmental community for over 20 years. With 97% of bay habitat in San Diego lost to development and the remainder much degraded over time because of commercial activities, this refuge will be managed to ensure that the bay's thousands of shorebirds and waterfowl migrating along the Pacific Flyway, as well as its resident species, will survive into the next century. Despite the dredging and filling of natural areas, many species of birds continue to frequent the Mission Bay area in the natural vegetation of the San Diego Flood Control Channel between Interstate 5 and the Pacific Ocean. A frontage road and bicycle paths offer prime viewing of this 200-acre preserve from both sides of the channel.

Wetlands are recognized as a very important ecosystem with functions and values such as biological diversity. This is when wetlands provide important habitat for diverse communities of plants and animals, including over 50 percent of the federally listed threatened or endangered species. Then there are waterfowl

habitats. Wetlands provide the principal habitat for migratory waterfowl. There are fisheries where wetlands provide direct spawning and rearing habitats and food supply that supports both freshwater and marine fisheries. Flood control is also included where flood flows are detained reducing the size of its destruction. Water quality plays a role in wetlands. This absorbs and filters pollutants that could otherwise degrade ground water or the water quality of rivers, lakes, and estuaries. Also wetlands provide recreation such as fishing, hunting and outdoor recreation.

Although there are many values that wetlands serve to improve the environment, there are also controversies that follow. The issue of hunting is very important. There are duck clubs that own many wetlands for people to shoot and kill birds. However, the duck hunters support and own the majority of the wetland habitat in California. Wetlands used to be seen as a breeding ground for disease-carrying mosquitoes. This is also a major factor in the flaws of wetlands. There are also a vast amount of endangered species that inhabit the waters of San Diego.

Bird Habitat: San Diego Boat Channel

The Boat Channel provides refuge for many species of waterfowl. This is partly because of the fact that San Diego Bay, specifically the Boat Channel, used to be a natural wetland before the introduction of industrialization. It is instinctual for many birds to flock to wetlands to seek suitable refuge during the migration and mating periods during a bird's lifespan. Even though the Boat Channel is no longer considered a natural wetland it still provides much of the same accommodations as one.

The Boat Channel is partly isolated from human activities due to its obscure location in the San Diego Bay. This region supports some of the highest bird diversity in the northern section of San Diego Bay. The lack of human interaction is perfect for the development of the bird's life. It allows the birds an unadulterated habitat to raise their young and occupy during the migratory seasons. All the required necessities are there, from habitat to feeding, and the birds must not be affected by the few negatives, human interaction and planes. It is amazing that so many birds find peace here directly underneath the take off flight path. It is likely

so many birds flock to the Boat Channels because the advantages outweigh the negatives so that the birds no longer pay heed to them.

Dolphin Mine Training

The Marine Mammal Program of the Navy began in 1959. The Navy was very interested in studying the hydrodynamics of dolphins. The initial benefit would be to improve torpedo, submarine, and ship design; however, the Navy soon discovered that dolphins have other resourceful qualities.

There are several Marine Mammal Systems for dolphin training used by the military. The MK4 system is used to find mines that are tethered to the ocean floor. The MK7 system is used to find mines that are on the ocean floor or buried in sediment. The dolphins also clear a path for human divers and equipment in this system. The MK8 system uses the dolphins and their trainers to find safe passages for troops to land.

Dolphins are utilized for this dangerous work because of their echolocation capabilities. Their radar sensors are more accurate than the Navy's technology, which makes locating mines easier. Dolphins are also able to make numerous deep dives without the side effects a human diver would suffer, as well as being a good alternative when a diving mission is too dangerous for a human to complete.

Dolphins are trained primarily by hand signals and positive reinforcement. If a dolphin performs a maneuver correctly, he will get a reward, such as fish or a whistle. A game or toy can also serve as a reward. There is also a clicker method that is effective for training dolphins. The clicker functions as a reward for the dolphin. A click will only be given when a trick or command is completed correctly.

Part of the dolphin mine training is happening in San Diego. The Navy utilizes Shelter Island and the Boat Channel for their dolphin training. The dolphins live in areas of the bay that are sectioned off for their use. These are convenient locations because of the proximity to Fort Rosecrans and MCRD.

Biogeography

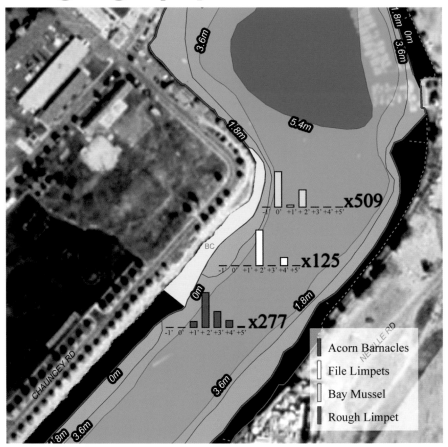

The above map displays a portion of the Boat Channel where the biodiversity survey was conducted. The area in yellow is the approximate extent of the survey transects. The flat bar graphs on the image above represent the abundance of the four most common species arranged by tide heights. The bar on the far left is the abundance of creatures at a -1 foot tide height while the bar on the far right is the abundance at a +5 foot tide height. The highest count per creature was set as the 100% mark and the other bars were scaled to match that. As a result, the graphs are not proportionate to each other. A scale factor is immediately to the right of the graph. For example, a scale of x227 means that the maximum value of that one graph is a count of 227 creatures per square meter.

Tide Height and Species Distribution at The Boat Channel

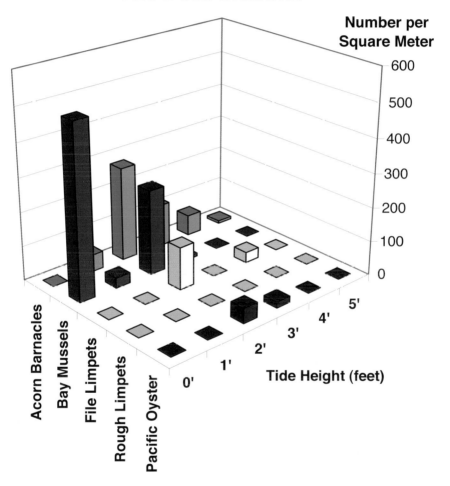

The above 3D graph represents the abundance of a certain species at a certain tide height. In the Boat Channel, acorn barnacles and mussels are the most common and appear in the lower tidal elevations from 0 feet to 3 feet. There were also an unusually large number of file limpets found at the 2 foot tide height. No rough limpets were found at this site.

SPANISH LANDING

History of The Spanish Landing

In 1542, Juan Rodriguez Cabrillo sailed from Mexico in search of a Northwest Passage. This hoped-for passage would allow traders to quickly travel from the Atlantic to the Pacific Ocean in pursuit of the Spice Islands, saving them a trip around the tip of South America. On September 28, 1542, Cabrillo found shelter in the bay of San Diego, a port he called San Miguel. Sixty years later the Spanish government sent Sebastian Vizcaino to revisit and explore the California Coast. He anchored off Point Loma and renamed the port of San Miguel, giving it the name used today, San Diego. He chose the name after the saint San Diego de Alcala. (Early Exploration 1999)

In 1768, Spain's interest in California was rekindled when Russian fur traders began moving into Southern California. As a result, King Carlos III of Spain gave

The historic location of the Spanish Landing marks one of the early Spanish entrances into California as well as the entrance to the present day Boat Channel. Ultimately, the Spaniards who landed here nearly 200 years ago would not be able to recognize the place today, nor would they believe the impact they had on the future of San Diego.

orders to occupy California. He issued these orders to Jose Galvez of Mexico to organize a party and explore the bays of San Diego and Monterey. Father Junipero Serra and Gaspar de Portola were given the task of making routes by land and sea. De Portola was to be the leader of the expedition and Father Serra was to be the leader for the missionaries. The plan was to first settle an establishment in San Diego and then move north to Monterey. (Spanish Landing 2005)

In early 1869, two ships were readied by Father Serra and Portola to leave the city of La Paz for the San Diego Bay. The San Antonio set off first and a month afterwards was followed by the San Carlos. On April 11, 1869, after a fifty-five day voyage, the San Carlos made its way into San Diego. Many of the crewmembers were sick and suffering from scurvy. Nevertheless, they could only lay anchor and wait for the late San Antonio to arrive. They set up camp on the beach and found

fresh water to replenish themselves. Men continued to die day after day as they waited another three weeks for the other ship to arrive. Two weeks later the San Antonio arrived even though it had started off a month earlier than the San Carlos. Its voyage had lasted one hundred ten days. Twenty-four men aboard the vessel had also died from scurvy. With this expedition of de Portola and Serra, began the Spanish occupation of Alta California. Today the Spanish Landing serves as a tribute to this historic event. (Mission History 2003)

Uses

At first glance, Spanish Landing Park looks just like an ordinary picnic area. A simple strip of beachfront land lined with grass and sidewalks, Spanish Landing Park seems limited to exactly what its name states, a park. However, there are many points of interest in and around Spanish Landing that one may overlook. The bay view from the park is gorgeous. Located across from the San Diego International Airport, one can bask in the sun and revel at the glory of the bay as majestic planes fly overhead and grand ships move lazily across the water. Whether one enjoys grass, large rocks, or sandy beaches, Spanish Landing Park caters to all.

The park is not limited to picnics and sightseeing. For bikers, Spanish Landing Park provides a trail just for biking. Using this trail, the casual or professional biker can enjoy the sport of cycling without worrying about pedestrians or cars. For those with children, there are numerous playgrounds that are safe for all ages. Restroom facilities are strategically placed along the length of the park. In addition to the picnic facilities, there are many restaurants around Spanish Landing Park. The options range from seafood at the Atlantis Restaurant, Italian food at Alfiere Mediterranean Bistro, to fast food at McDonalds.

At various times during the year, visitors can catch one of the many activities hosted at Spanish Landing. For example, there is the Annual San Diego Cajun Zydeco Music and Food Festival, the Annual Wells Fargo San Diego International Triathlon, Mardi Gras parties, and many more events for all types of people (San Diego Calendar of Events).

Location

The Spanish Landing, generally referred to as "Spanish Landing Park," is located off Harbor Drive in downtown San Diego. It sits between Point Loma and San Diego at the mouth of the Boat Channel. It is on the southwest end of the former Naval Training Center and is only a short distance from the San Diego Airport. Spanish Landing is a considerable distance from the harbor entrance and situated where the bay turns inward. From  its shore visitors get a great view of both the San Diego cityscape as well as the Bay itself. The Spanish Landing is considered to be the historical arrival site of the Portola-Serra Expedition from Spain that occurred in 1896.

Sources

"Spanish Landing." Crone's Cobblestone Cottage. 7 May 2005
       <http://www.cobblestonebandb.com/bed_breakfast/891_spanish_land
       ing.html>
Hughart, Kathy, and Bill White. "Early Exploration of San Diego." 1999.
       California History & Culture Conservancy. 7 May 2005.
       <http://historyandculture.com/chcc/explorers.html>.
Mission History. 12 May 2005
       <http://www.missionsandiego.com/mission_history.htm>.

Description and Feeling

At the mouth of the San Diego Boat Channel is a strip of bay called the Spanish Landing. Here the Channel and the waters of the bay are separated by the Boat Channel Bridge which connects Point Loma to the San Diego mainland. The view is very unique. Beautiful green trees and passing cars in the background mix an urban setting with a natural one. There is a concrete boardwalk, sections of grass, juniper trees, and wooden benches. It is a pretty place to hang out during the day, but at times its pleasant environment can be interrupted by the sound of zooming traffic and planes flying overhead. Despite the noise, many people flock to the region to have picnics with their friends and family, or to stroll along the boardwalk when the weather is nice. There isn't much wildlife at Spanish Landing, but occasionally birds pass by and take a swim in the water in order to escape the hot beams of the sun. Spanish Landing is a great place for relaxation because the view of downtown and blue waters makes the scene look like a postcard.

Only a Scrawny Bird

As part of his daily routine,
The old weathered seaman notes
It's about time for lunch; there's a lack of shadows on the
water

Adorned with tough waterproof yellow
And blue boot-like feet to protect him
As he ventures through the knee-deep tide

Slick silvery fish are no match for his skill
Without need of a skillet, fire, or pan
He slides the prisoner down his throat
Carefully avoiding his scraggly grandfather beard.

—Megan MacLaggan

Biology of the Spanish Landing

Shady Places

In the murk and muck of the Spanish Landing, we spot color—a glimmer of orange in the vastness of green eelgrass and brown mud. Upon closer examination, this strange creature is a slug, or more specifically a nudibranch. These shell-less, jelly-bodied snails can be found in many colors and many shapes. They use opposite ends of the evolutionary spectrum to defend themselves. Some are colored a murky brown and green to perfectly blend with their surroundings, while others are bright neon oranges and blues to alert any fish that it is deadly poisonous.

The nudibranches of the Spanish Landing are found in the shallow and intertidal zones where they can find protection as well as food. Some live in the eelgrasses where they consume sponges, hydroids, bryozoans, tunicates, barnacles, and even other nudibranches. Since the bodies of these creatures are extremely soft, they must hide from predators in nice shady locations. There is a tendency for intertidal nudibranches to be found in shady spots. The most common explanation relates to the bizarre reproduction methods of the nudibranch. All nudibranches are hermaphroditic, which means they possess both male and female sex organs. While self-fertilization is extremely rare, it increases the chances of finding a mate. When nudibranches lay eggs, they almost always leave them in the darkest, shadiest spot they can find – hence the tendency towards the dark. If one is to hunt for a nudibranch, look for the brightly colored slug in the shady areas of the intertidal zones.

Interactions of the Spanish Landing

The Homeless of the Spanish Landing

We have observed many forms of life being pushed out of their environment by human development. At the same time, many individuals of our own kind have been cast out from our civilized society. Those without a home know they are not wanted, so they hide from astonishing cruelty put forth by the affluent members of our society. Law enforcement on Coronado Island makes an effort to keep the streets free of vagrants and vagabonds. No homeless have been seen living on the pleasant sands of Scripps Beach. Instead, they have found safe haven in the parks of the Spanish Landing, beneath the boat channel bridge, and along the muddy banks of the boat channel.

The park, which offers a beautiful jogging and bicycling trail, also has grass and shade trees for tired wanderers. Food left over from picnics provides an opportunity for the transients to scavenge. The park also has restroom facilities. These are locked up at night, but are available for use by any passers-by during daylight hours. All those without a regular roof over their heads are living under difficult circumstances, but some of the homeless people seem to be better fed than others. This could be an example of survival of the fittest. Those who have perfected the technique of "bumming" can get more out of the unforgiving environment they live in. Some homeless can even claim to have beachfront residences. Living on the beaches of San Diego can't be that unforgiving.

Not even the best adapted transient can withstand the terrible forces of nature that strike the bay, the city, and all of San Diego County. During the 2005 San Diego rain storms, many of these people had to find a roof quickly. Perhaps some could not find the shelter they needed, and were left to shiver in the cold rain. Some areas were flooded, and some people could have been trapped. Not all roofs in San Diego are insulated, something that most of us take for granted. When it isn't raining, living outside in the hot sun puts the homeless in danger of sunburns, dehydration, and overheating. These are the environmental conditions that the homeless must adapt to without the help of air conditioning, heating, or filtered water. Pushed away from these modern developments, the homeless of San Diego live a unique, almost wild existence.

Biogeography

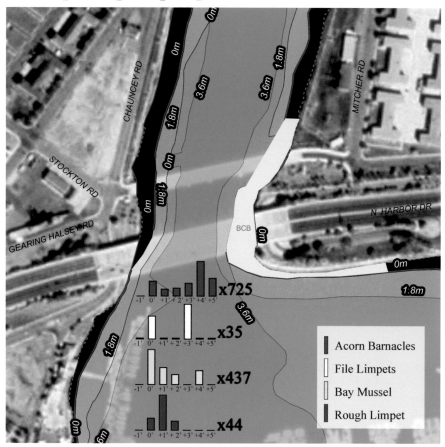

The above map displays a portion of the Spanish Landing where the biodiversity survey was conducted. The area in yellow is the approximate extent of the survey transects. The flat bar graphs on the image above represent the abundance of the four most common species arranged by tide heights. The bar on the far left is the abundance of creatures at a -1 foot tide height while the bar on the far right is the abundance at a +5 foot tide height. The highest count per creature was set as the 100% mark and the other bars were scaled to match that. As a result, the graphs are not proportionate to each other. A scale factor is immediately to the right of the graph. For example, a scale of x227 means that the maximum value is 227 times larger than a set constant.

Tide Height and Species Distribution at The Spanish Landing

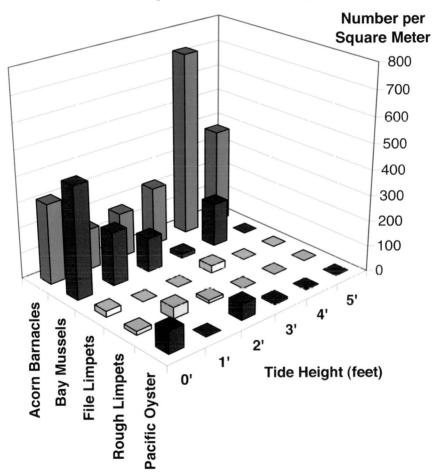

The above 3D graph represents the abundance of a certain species at a certain tide height. The Spanish landing had an overall large number of creatures, especially barnacles and mussels; these creatures were found at virtually every tide height in great numbers. Much like the other survey sites, however, the mussels had a tendency to be more common in the lower tidal heights. This site had some of the largest creature counts for +4 and +5 tide heights.

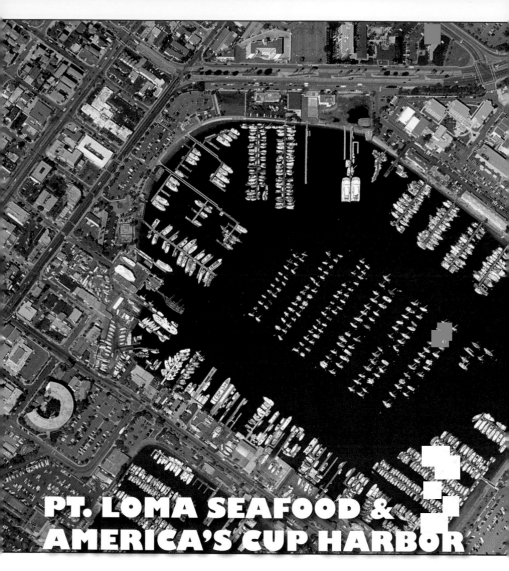

PT. LOMA SEAFOOD & AMERICA'S CUP HARBOR

History of Point Loma Seafood

Point Loma Seafood has a fascinating history. It opened its doors to enthusiastic and curious customers in 1963. The store was the manifested dream of Kelly Christianson, who started displaying fresh fish in a small case out of an even smaller store. Christianson's determination and focus on providing great seafood made his store unique and remarkable. He was so concerned with the quality of his products he would hand pick the freshest catches to sell in his store. His efforts, along with the help of his sons and his wife, built Point Loma Seafood as well as a great reputation, setting them apart from all the other seafood markets. Soon the store was filled with customers and success was inevitable. The menu extends to the various smoked or processed fish, crabs, lobster, shrimp and squid. (Point Loma Seafood, 2005)

Good food and good entertainment make for a good combination. This harbor is dedicated to the ever more popular sport of sailboat racing while a local restaurant dedicates itself to fulfilling the appetites of the many sea-oriented people in the area. These places attract many people, many fishing boats, and hence many birds. While the intertidal life in the bay may be somewhat lacking, the diversity and quantity of seabirds is astounding.

The success of the seafood store led to the development of the restaurant. Warm seafood was first made and eaten only by the employees of Point Loma Seafood. After becoming famous among the workers, great seafood became available to all customers. Christianson's standards of quality were carried out and the hot, fresh fish was served on the freshest sourdough bread with a state of the art tartar sauce. As the years went by the local customers grew and so did the restaurant. Although the building was renovated, the tradition stayed the same. The freshest thing in town is the only thing served at the Point Loma Seafood restaurant. (Point Loma Seafood, 2005)

History of the America's Cup Harbor

The America's Cup is actually one of the oldest sports ever held that still exists today. This historical event has been around for more than 150 years. The history of the America's Cup began on August 22nd, 1851 during the Great Exhibition of London.

The race was inaugurated by Queen Victoria at the Isle of Wight. The outcome resulted in USA's victory. The winning American team donated their prize to the New York Yacht Club (NYYC). This "Deed of Gift" was the beginning of what America's Cup stands for. Aside from being the oldest race in history, it is also the oldest race rewarding trophies as prizes. (America's Cup 2005)

The United States has won the America's Cup many times, including twice bringing the Cup to our shores. The first time was in 1851, as noted above. Then, after many successful defenses, the United States lost the Cup to Australia in 1983. For the 1987 event, the nearby San Diego Yacht Club entered its Stars & Stripes team, who won the Cup in Fremantle, Western Australia. The United States, via the San Diego Yacht Club, successfully defended the Cup in both the 1988 and 1992 competitions held in the ocean waters west of Point Loma. However, in 1995 the United States lost the Cup to New Zealand. Today, in memory of America's Cup races, the harbor near Shelter Island is known as the America's Cup Harbor. (America's Cup, 2005).

Uses

Point Loma Seafood is located at the Fisherman's Landing area of Point Loma. This is yet another popular visiting spot, complete with a wide variety of attractions. With dozens of boats docked in its harbor, Point Loma Seafood offers a great deal of excitement. The area offers recreational services, such as harbor and fishing boat tours, and boat rentals. For those looking to find a quality meal in this area, the Point Loma Seafood Restaurant offers outstanding food and a seating area that looks over the beautiful America's Cup Harbor. The long walking path along the shore winds its way past many restaurants, dock and gift shops, offering a peaceful retreat.

On any day of the week, visitors are able to witness the workings of the local fishermen. For the majority of the day, the area is used as an unloading area for fishermen. The daily catch of fish brought from the ocean is tossed onto the cement above the docks by fishing boat crew members, providing an unusual sight for visitors. With all of its unique attractions, Point Loma Seafood is top choice for those deciding on a place to visit along San Diego's amazing harbor.

Location

Point Loma Seafood is located just west of Rosecrans street in the Point Loma area of San Diego, California. Point Loma Seafood is a popular spot in Point Loma. From the restaurant one can look out on the America's Cup Harbor. Just beyond Point Loma Seafood, one can see the tip of Shelter Island and farther out one can see Coronado Island. Point Loma Seafood and the America's Cup Harbor are down from the Marine Physical Lab, which is closer to the Harbor's entrance. While Shelter Island extends before it, Point Loma Seafood's location hugs the side of Point Loma's sunset cliffs. The location of Point Loma Seafood gives visitors access to the Bay, America's Cup Harbor, Shelter Island and many businesses located on the street of Rosecrans.

Sources

"Point Loma Sport Fishing." TECK.net.5 June 2005
        <http://www.pointlomasportfishing.com >.

"Shelter Island Point." Pacifica Hotel Company. 5 May 2005
        <www.shelterpointe.com>.

"Point Loma Seafood." Point Loma Seafood. 25 May 2005.
        <www.plsf.com/history.html>

Johnson, Jon J. "Americas Cup". America's Cup History. 9 May 2005
        <http://www.newzealand.com/travel/sights-activities/events-calendar
/americas-cup-feature/about-americas-cup/americas-cup-history.cfm>.

Description and Feeling

The market is busy today with the smell of freshly caught fish lingering in the air. I pull a number and join in with the rest of the bustling bodies. I order the usual, tuna grilled sandwich with a side of french fries. My hands dig deeply into my pockets, pulling out eight dollars for my order. I move on with the line. I stand and watch the preparation of fresh fish, waiting for my number to be called. The dull gleam of the steel knife entrances me as it glides through the flesh effortlessly, with such precision and speed. In minutes what used to be a whole fish is now reduced to pink fillets, ready to be cooked and eaten. I hear my order being called in the background, "Number 36!" The call brings me back to my senses.

Walking outside of the restaurant, my stomach content and full, I notice a change in scenery. Various boats, from little to big, make the view extravagant. Peeking up, I see clear skies, without any sight of grey clouds. Being outside does not bring a single moment of discomfort. With every second of the day a refreshing breeze brushes my face and whispers in my ears. As I step down closer to the tides, I discover a world of unknown creatures hidden in their niches. I have gone from complacently walking along the sidewalk to the eager explorations of what the receding tide has revealed.

A Sign of Power

Gazing upon an open ocean
Wondering what's all the commotion
People throwing rocks trying to hit the pipe
But all I can see is the water in motion

Also, the sign atop the pipe is about to fall
If it came crashing down it would be a really close call
As if the hand of god was making a decision
Making even the most powerful man feel so small

—Ross Zafar

As Free as a Bird
A Nature Reflection by Jon Smith

As I lie along the shore, my mind winds in every direction. I watch as life moves at light speed. People are racing, wind is blowing, birds are flying, and I take it all in. Usually I can't sit still. I begin to feel like I'm wasting my time and I have to move. But things are different here. I find my life has meaning, and therefore I can take a break from it and just reflect.

The one thing that keeps catching my eye are the birds. They can fly and dart every which way. How is it that birds can fly, but humans cannot? Aren't we superior? The birds are so graceful, gathering food and just living. Someday I hope that I can just live. I won't have to worry about school, work, anything. Someday I want to be a bird, I envy their freedom.

Are there any humans that resemble these birds? Everyone seems so wrapped up in their self-righteous ambitions that they forget to live. They waste their lives gathering as much wealth and junk as possible before they die. When they do go, everything they have earned is suddenly meaningless. People need to realize that there is more to life than just material wealth.

The people that resemble birds the most are most likely the homeless. But even they are flawed. How many of them chose that way of life? Most of them have drowned themselves in drugs and alcohol, until they have nothing left. There are only a select few who truly see the beauty in being free. I hope that someday I will see the light. I feel as though I know this now, but that's hard to say, since I'm only a little shy of seventeen. I can't wait until I can honestly say that I am a bird.

Interactions of America's Cup Harbor

Effect of Copper and Tin-Based Boat Paints on Marine Life at Point Loma Seafood

The ancient Greeks were the first to use copper on their boats. They used copper to prevent fouling of the hull by encrusting invertebrates. The Ancient Greeks also used lead sheathing to protect the hull of their boats. The Greeks, however, did not realize that the copper polluted the ocean and marine life.

Historically copper and tin have been used to prevent barnacles from living on the hull of a ship. The copper- and tin-based paint used on the boats anchored at the America's Cup Harbor harms the marine life. This is due to the fact that this copper and tin is very lethal to the animal's health. The problem with this method is that the barnacles die from the copper and tin instead of just being repelled by it.

A big controversy is going on right now between the boat industry and environmentalists. The boat industry wants to use copper and tin based paint on their ships because it is cheaper. The environmentalists want the use of copper- and tin-based paint banned because it harms the environment and the marine life that lives near the ships. Copper and tin based paint also pollutes and contaminates the water. The paint can also harm humans when they eat seafood from the ocean that is contaminated.

Tribuyltin is an extremely controversial and dangerous contaminant that is being used in our oceans today, in the form of paint. The paints, which have been used for forty years by the shipping industry to repair hull damage and reduce drag, last for about 5 to 6 years. The shipping industry likes to use the copper- and tin-based paint because it is relatively inexpensive. The chemicals that seep out of the paint contaminate the water. Mollusks have been used as indicators for recognizing TBT pollution because they are extremely sensitive to the chemicals released by the paint, and chemicals from the paint also affect clams and oysters.

There have been many new advances in the quest to develop new anti-fouling paints through technological advances that have originated from the paint industry. Although these new paints are considered to be "eco friendly" because they are tin-free, they contain high concentrations of zinc, copper and other toxic biocides. The problem with these new paints is that they tend to be a lot more expensive than the harmful copper- and tin-based paints. There are companies such as Poseidon that see the future of antifouling paints in non-toxic paints.

The Sea Lion and the Fishermen

While the relationship between the fisherman and sea lions may seem nothing but friendly, many people do not realize the hardships the animals endure when out at sea. Sea lions are often seen lazily swimming throughout America's Cup Harbor, frequently being fed by local fishermen. While in the San Diego harbor, the sea lions may be no more than a tourist attraction, but when out at sea, they are the fisherman's biggest competition.

Sea lions were hunted along the California Islands from 1800 to around 1860. As the sea lion hunting industry grew, the animal's population rapidly dropped. By the early 1900's there were less than 1,500 recorded California sea

lions. The Marine Animal Protection Act, enacted in 1972, gave protection to species that have been heavily hunted. Because of this program, the population of California sealions has grown to over 160,000.

With the growing fishing industry covering most of California's waters, the sea lions habitat is constantly threatened. Fishing boats frequently report large numbers of sea lions caught and killed in fishing nets. In 1999 a recorded 533 marine animals were killed in fishing nets. The majority of these marine species were California sea lions .

Nearly 8% of sea lions rescued by the Marine Mammal Center in Sausalito, California suffer from gun shot wounds. sea lions pose a great threat to fishing boats' catch. The animals often hunt and scare off groups of fish that may be hunted by fishermen. In order to reduce the competition for a catch, fishermen often go as far as to kill the sea lions . Fishermen also try to deter sea lions from an area by using "sealbombs," devices that produce small explosions in the water in order to scare away Sea Lions. Sea Lions often go deaf after repeated encounters with these bombs. If the animals come too close to the device, they may be killed.

The cruel methods of reducing fishing competition used by fishermen, are a major factor in the depletion of the California Sea Lion population. Laws such as the Marine Mammal Protection Act of 1972 help to sustain the amount of sea lions living in California. Many American fishermen are currently working to destroy such acts so that they are able to kill sea lions without prosecution. If the public does not become aware of the sea lion's safety issues, the species may be in great danger.

The Sport Fishing Industry's Effect on the Wildlife

Point Loma Seafood is located on America's Cup Harbor near the San Diego Bay. The location of Point Loma Seafood is a natural tourist attraction which is the main source of human activity within this area. One thing this area boasts is the sport fishing industry. Point Loma Seafood grabs the attention of fishermen, sport fishing boats and other sailors looking for a new harbor as their home. This constant and rapidly increasing human activity affects the wildlife in this area, especially the marine life of the adjoining San Diego Bay. There are several sport fishing events conducted in the Point Loma area near the San Diego Bay that sponsor and encourage this activity.

An example of one of these sport fishing activities is the San Diego 26th Annual Day at the Docks that was held on Sunday, April 24th, 2005 at Point Loma. This is a special event in which the San Diego Sport Fishing Council sponsors a showcase of San Diego sport fishing. Tourists and San Diegans are invited to experience and learn about the art of sport fishing.

While this activity is great fun, its byproducts are drastically affecting the marine organisms in the Bay. More and more fish and other marine life creatures are being caught by these fishermen, causing a decrease in species populations. This is bad for the environment and the health of the marine life because it may lead to overfishing or even the extinction of a certain type of fish or other aquatic creature. Though there are many negative affects of the sport fishing industry, there are some positive affects.

Sport fishing can also be observed in a positive way. Though it may seem that sport fishermen are hurting the fish, they are actually helping the fish. Sport fishermen have to pay for their fishing licenses to sport fishing organizations. These sport fishing organizations give back to the fish community by creating reserves and protected areas for the fish to prevent fishing in that area. Therefore, the sport fishermen are actually helping the fish by sport fishing. The economic impact of recreational fishing adds up to 116 billion dollars. So fishermen are helping the economy and the fish. The money the fishermen use to buy their fishing licenses is used by sport fishing industries and the government to help protect the fish and other aquatic creatures.

Biogeography

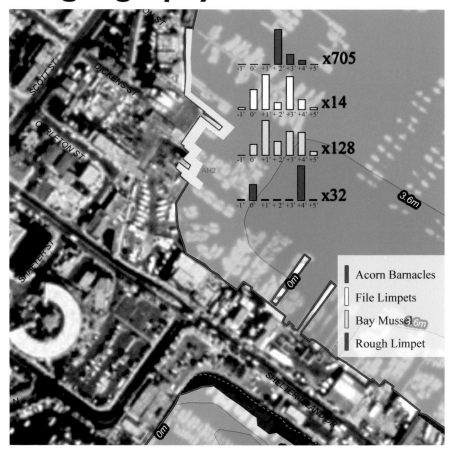

The above map displays a portion of Point Loma Seafood in America's Cup Harbor where the biodiversity survey was conducted. The area in yellow is the approximate extent of the survey transects. The flat bar graphs on the image above represent the abundance of the four most common species arranged by tide heights. The bar on the far left is the abundance of creatures at a -1 foot tide height while the bar on the far right is the abundance at a +5 foot tide height. The highest count per creature was set as the 100% mark and the other bars were scaled to match that. As a result, the graphs are not proportionate to each other. A scale factor is immediately to the right of the graph.

Tide Height and Species Distribution at Point Loma Seafood

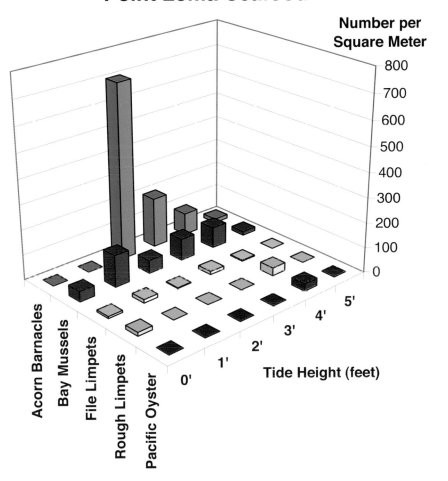

The above 3D graph represents the abundance of a certain species at a certain tide height. Most of the animals found near Point Loma Seafood in America's Cup harbor were barnacles. There was not a lot of biodiversity and only small numbers of other species. There was a layer of barnacles in large numbers once the +2' tide height was reached. A steady spread of mussels was another common trend throughout the survey site.

SHELTER ISLAND

History of Shelter Island

The area around what was to become the man-made island known as Shelter Island was, as early as 1859, referred to as a "shoal or mudbank." Around 1934, Shelter Island began to be built out of this mudbank to widen the mouth of the bay. The main entrance to the Bay became a popular location for dredging, so that Navy aircraft carriers could sail into the San Diego Port. "Shelter Island," named for protection to boats and yachts, was built out of this dredging material. Upon its completion, Shelter Island was introduced to the community in 1937, when ladies on the entertainment committee of San Diego Yacht Club decided to host a beach barbeque there. ("Scalon" 2005)

In the shelter of an island with marinas, res-taurants, parks, hotels, beaches, stores, and parking lots, what life still clings to rocks and the sands between the tides? The answer is surprising and broad. With many different species and drastic biodiversity changes throughout the island this place is always a wonder.

      As part of San Diego's huge Navy presence, the Navy decided to make use of Shelter Island. During World War II, a couple of ammunition magazines houses were placed on the north end of the island. A keeper at Ballast Point Lighthouse reported in the years after World War II, that a storm washed away all evidence of the Navy's presence on the island. He knew this to be true because some of the Navy's Shelter Island possessions washed up on the Ballast Point beach. Finally in 1948, efforts were made to connect the island to the main land by dividing the yacht basin with a 2,150-foot-long and 250-foot-wide causeway. People began living on the island in 1953. Over the years businesses were built. Today Shelter Island includes several hotels, marine businesses, and restaurants. ("Evolution of San Diego Playground" 2005; "Shelter Island, Harbor Island" 2005)

Uses

Shelter Island has many uses, including yacht businesses, marinas, restaurants, hotels, recreation, and tourism. Shelter Island has a small residential area, even though there are not many private homes on the island. Shelter Island businesses include boating and yachting facilities. These businesses can do everything from selling or renting to repairing boats. In addition to the boating businesses, there are many sport fishing and tackle shops. These places sell anything needed to satisfy a fisherman's needs. Shelter Island's location on the Bay makes it an ideal location for marine businesses.

Shelter Island is also a great recreational area. There is a large boat launch frequently used by the public. In addition, a beautiful boardwalk stretches the length of the island and goes right along the water. This pathway is an excellent spot to take a walk in the morning. (Another nice feature of this pathway is that dogs are allowed to join their master's walk.) The boardwalk is very clean with hardly any trash, the lawns are well maintained, the landscaping is well kept, and the concrete path is barely chipped or damaged. Along the pathway, there is a fishing pier that can't be missed and a public restroom right across from it. The pier is made of wood and is a spot where many fishermen go to try to catch fish. Right after the fishing pier, there is a small playground off to the side. It has a set of swings, a play structure, and a pair of huge plastic turtles.

Shelter Island is also the West Coast's largest public celebration of sport fishing and is home to an annual festival called the Day at the Docks. The Day at the Docks festival reminds San Diego just how important sport fishing is to many people.

Shelter Island is a huge year-round tourist spot, with many hotels and restaurants. Humphrey's Half Moon Inn and Suites is one hotel that is facing the bay and has excellent views. The Bali Hai restaurant also has a nice view of the bay and spectacular view of downtown. Besides having restaurants and hotels for tourists, a hybrid sea land bus goes right around the island and eventually dives into the water for a scenic and unique tour.

There are many activities to do and many things to see at Shelter Island. Shelter Island is never quiet or boring. It's a great place to come check out while visiting San Diego.

Location

Shelter Island is a small, man-made island located off Canon Street in Point Loma. The man-made island juts out like a large "T" and is just southwest of the San Diego International Airport. The Island is surrounded by the San Diego Bay and is connected to the northern part of Point Loma by a causeway. The island is about two miles long from the mouth of San Diego Bay. Shelter Island is right across from the North Island Naval Air Station on Coronado Island. It lies about a quarter mile off the coast and is approximately one mile long. Shelter Island is close to many other important parts of San Diego including Fort Rosecrans, Cabrillo National Monument, and Liberty Station, the former Naval Training Center (NTC). Shelter Island provides its visitors with a tremendous view of the towering office, hotel, and apartment buildings of downtown San Diego.

Sources

"Shelter Island, Scanlon, Karen" The Log 23 May 2005
        <http://www.thelog.com/special/specialview.asp?c=75584>.

"Evolution of San Diego's Playground." Karen Scanlon 23 May 2005
        <http://www.thelog.com/special/specialview.asp?c=75583>.

"Shelter Island, Harbor Island." San Diego CVB 23 May 2005
        <http://www.magazineusa.com/cityguide/ca_sandiego/c_s_harborisland.asp>.

Description and Feeling

I walk through Point Loma passing marine shops, yachting offices, restaurants and more. There are many people wandering around this beautiful location. As I continue walking, the view in front of me becomes spectacular. The sunshine reflects brightly off of the San Diego Bay water making it hard to stare forward.

The sun is beating right down on my face. I am sitting on a fishing dock that moves slightly as the water moves about. There are ducks swimming in this little alcove and birds flying above. A big brown pelican swoops low to the water every now and then looking for fish. I hear an occasional duck quack and an occasional squawk from a seagull. I hear trucks behind me, boats in front of me, and airplanes above me. There are military helicopters flying around and boats sailing in and out of this boating area. Right now, at this very moment, I see a seal swimming in this cove area. It is really close to me and coming closer. I am so close to

it I can see its ears and water dripping off its silky skin. I can see its cute face and long whiskers. I am so close to touching it but as I reach out to it, a boat starts its roaring engine and scares the sea lion. The sea lion dives underwater and within seconds I see its head pop up a long way away. It's left the cove.

Return to Just the Same
A Nature Reflection by Michael Dresser

Glistening water, seagulls, moss, and seaweed-covered rocks, boats, trash, buildings and waves. There are a lot of boats. Students scattered along the coast. There are birds flying; birds are walking along the shore. I smell an air so familiar that it's no longer recognizable. I hear an engine running, possibly a generator or water craft, but not a boat. Green rocks, visually damp from where the shore line used to appear. I see fishing line, bottles and boxes scattered along the rocks.

One particular rock in the water is covered in seaweed like all the others but there is an odd growth on its side. I am unsure what it is. Waves rhythmically collide on this one particular rock. "Why is it here?" These are all questions I ask myself to which there is no answer. At times the water glistens and makes it harder to look at the rock. The waves increase, splashing higher on the rock. The seaweed, exposed to the sun, dries and withers in the powerful heat

My gaze moves beyond the intermediate shore; I spot a bright red or orange stationary buoy that bobs up and down. There is no evident purpose, though I'm sure it shows ships how to safely pass. As variances in the wind kick up the water, the orange ball just sits there bobbing, without a care in the world. It leads the army of boats as if a commanding general was ensuring his troops stay in one line. It sits on the mouth of the docks subjected to all the element's punishments, but still it just sits.

I watch the waves approach and dissipate on the shore line and I watch the sand beneath the wave cloud up then settle down again. I watch what once was changed return just as fast to the same. The waves come in changing the once glassy smooth surface to that of chaos and uncertainty. Then in a matter of seconds, everything returns it to its once crystalline state of purity.

Two Worlds
There are two worlds coexisting on one planet
What was once one has become the other
I am torn between these two worlds
Nature and civilization.

We choose civilization to escape nature's beauty
Yet by doing so, we brutalize nature.
I long to escape all of brutality
But I don't know how.

—Will Gomez-Hicks

Biology of Shelter Island

Scavenger Seagulls

Shelter Island, located on the opposite side of the San Diego Bay from downtown San Diego, is where the waste of the bay is pushed ashore. Seagulls are attracted to it and seem to populate Shelter Island, freeloading on everything that ends up there. From roads signs to golf balls and sea squirts, the seagulls seem to love them all.

    Seagulls have the tendency to eat every-thing that looks edible. All the trash at Shelter Island seems to get the at-tention of all the seagulls. That's probably why there are so many. The trash comes from humans who throw it away into the bay. Companies, restaurants and boats release their waste into the bay. For example, when Bali High's restaurants dump their leftovers and scraps of food into the bay, the seagulls, having unlimited food, gather up and take whatever is dumped.

    One important reason why seagulls are at Shelter Island is because it's located on the bay. All kinds of fish live in the water for them to eat. One of the fishes would be the bait fish that fishers usually get. Tourists from around the world also love to sight-see at Shelter Island and feed the seagulls.

    Another example would be all the boats that sail in the bay. The humans on them throw their trash and waste into the bay. First it pollutes the water, and then it gets pushed ashore onto beaches like Shelter Island. Nothing else is

at Shelter Island for the seagulls to eat but some sea squirts, which are too deep to get, and acorn barnacles, which aren't edible for seagulls. So the logical reason why so many seagulls are at Shelter Island would be the trash and scraps that are thrown onto the bay from humans.

Interactions of Shelter Island

Pelicans and Fishermen

After returning from a long fishing trip, the fishermen at Shelter Island reward the pelicans with fresh fish guts. If it weren't for the pelicans, the fishermen wouldn't have been as successful as they were. Out on the water, the pelicans prove to be very helpful. Their keen sense and great eyesight helps spot fish, much like a hunting dog spots a bird. The fisherman pays a great deal of attention to the pelican's movements. Once a group of pelicans begins to circle and dive into the water frequently, the fisherman quickly moves to that area hoping to grab a bite. What is happening is that the pelican spots bait fish near the surface. The fisherman hopes that larger fish are pushing the bait to the surface.

When I was fishing in Mulege, Mexico I would always look out on the horizon hoping to catch a glimpse of a splash or a diving bird circling high above the water. Most of the trip we were not catching a thing. No birds and the fish just weren't biting. Once I caught a glimpse of birds circling high above; my adrenaline began to rush. I thought that I might finally fight a big fish. We gunned the engines and skipped over the waves, rushing to where the birds had been spotted. With the wind rushing through my hair I was no longer tired and hot from four hours in the hot sun. I was ready for whatever might happen next. Once we arrived at the spot, birds were diving near the boat. We set out the trolling lines and waited for a bite. Sure enough the line shot out and it was my turn to fight the fish. Almost every fisherman experiences the same scenario. If it weren't for the pelican the fisherman would be fishing blindly.

The relationship between pelicans and fishermen is similar to that of hunters and their dogs. When bird hunting, it is a huge advantage to have a smart well-trained dog. Dogs' keen sense of smell and eyesight gives the hunter an early warning system of when a bird is near. The hunter watches the dog's reactions and movements. When the dog freezes, the hunter knows where the bird is. The hunter treats the dog with respect much like the fisherman respects the pelican. When the fishermen come into port in San Diego they are met by pelicans looking for food and fish. As a token of respect the fishermen leave the guts, head, and other scraps of the fish for the pelicans.

Overall most fishermen see the pelican as the most experienced fisherman of the sea, and all fishermen respect it. Without it, fishermen would lose a valuable companion. They would lose their ability to know where the big fish are and above all they would never experience watching them circle high over the water.

Fishing at Shelter Island

Beside boating and sightseeing, fishing is also a common natural activity. One great place that you can go to fish is at the Shelter Island pier. At this location, fishing is an easy sport where you're bound to catch one of the common fish at the pier. These common fish include the halibut and the bass, but there have also been slight reports of catching bonita, perch, and calico. The pier is full of fishermen of all expertise, from the avid, who come almost every weeks, to the novices, who come once a month. Pier fishing doesn't always have to be done with a standard fishing pole. Many fishermen use a small net to try their luck, but the most interesting device used wasn't very advanced in technology. One could probably find all the needed materials in their home. This creative little device was made of a normal liter bottle, some string, and a hook. Although fishing skills are diverse, fishing is a great activity for people at Shelter Island who use their leisure time to get away for a brief vacation.

Fishing can be seen as a lonesome sport or the exact opposite. One can

use fishing for means of relaxing or to get away from the ordinary rush of life. It could also be used as a way to spend time and get closer to both friends and family. I guess it is something about fishing on the pier of Shelter Island that brings both tranquility and camaraderie to all who come. So it was slightly un-derstandable why some people felt a little disturbed when they were approached to contribute their experiences about fishing on the pier.

This activity is not only for means of relaxing, but it also brings along both fun and amusement. While at the pier we met Mary who we noticed was fishing with just some spool, a hook, and a liter bottle that she used to reel in her meal. When asked about her device, she said it has not given her any luck, but she still enjoys doing the sport. Mary visits the pier every Monday to bring a van of elderly veterans for a great day of fishing or navy boat watching. We also met Matt, who comes just about twice a week and from watching seemed to be very good. He told us about one of his awful days of fishing at the pier. He had just caught a good sized bass, and just as he was reeling it in a sea lion jumped up and took it off the hook, and that very same day he had caught a small fish and a bigger fish jumped right up out of the water and swallowed it. Fish are not the only creatures caught at the pier; there have been occasions when birds have been yanked from the sky. There was one incident when just as a fellow named John cast his pole out, he caught a pigeon by the tail with the hook, and had to reel it in as though he would a fish to save it. The most amusing was when a young gentleman by the name of Steve had accidentally lost his pole in the water, and the person next to him cast his out, too, and thought he had caught a fish. He had luckily caught the young gentleman's pole.

Pier fishing at Shelter Island is a great place for fun, relaxation, and also as a way to meet new people. This activity is a great way to be engulfed in nature, and at the same time still not be too far from the city. For the future try Mary's idea and come up with a new mechanism to better your chances at catching some of the common fish at the boat channel. At the same time try to not have bad karma and lose your fishing rod into the bay. Hopefully someone will retrieve it for you.

Biogeography

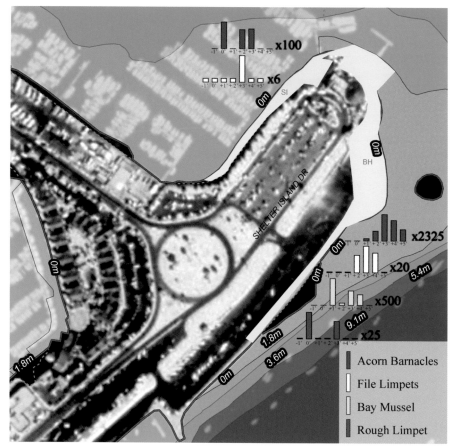

The above map displays a portion of Shelter Island where the biodiversity survey was conducted. The area in yellow is the approximate extent of the survey transects. The flat bar graphs on the image above represent the abundance of the four most common species arranged by tide heights. The bar on the far left is the abundance of creatures at a -1 foot tide height while the bar on the far right is the abundance at a +5 foot tide height. The highest count per creature was set as the 100% mark and the other bars were scaled to match that. As a result, the graphs are not proportionate to each other. A scale factor is immediately to the right of the graph. For example, a scale of x227 means that the maximum value is 227 times larger than a set constant.

Tide Height and Species Distribution at Bali Hai on Shelter Island

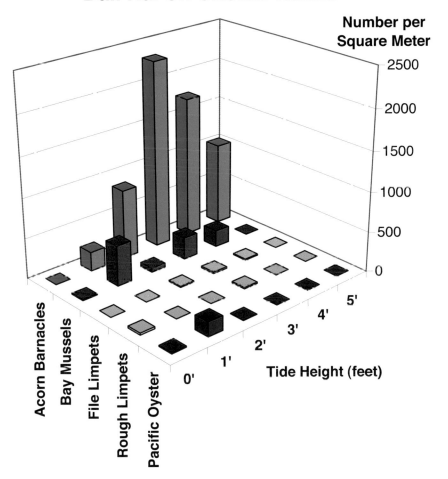

The above 3D graph represents the abundance of a certain species at a certain tide height. This study was conducted off of the shores of the Bali Hai restaurant on the northwestern tip of Shelter Island. This location had an extremely large number of creatures and lots of biodiversity. It is hard to tell this in the 3D graph however, because the vertical scale was blown out of proportion by the large volume of barnacles that were across the shore.

153

SCRIPPS FACILITY

History of the Scripps Facility

Scripps Institute of Oceanography was founded in 1903 by Professor William E. Ritter, from the University of California. At that time the research institute was named the Marine Biological Association of San Diego. The seaside laboratory was founded under the University of California's zoology program. The original laboratory was located in Coronado, and it wasn't until 1907 that it moved to where it is today at the end of Point Loma. In 1912, the Institute was renamed Scripps Institution for Biological Research. It wasn't until 1925 that it inherited the name it now has, Scripps Institute of Oceanography, Marine Physical Lab. ("History of SIO" 2005)

Thomas Wayland Vaughan took over as president after Professor Ritter retired in 1923. Vaughan had great expectations for the Institute. Vaughan planned

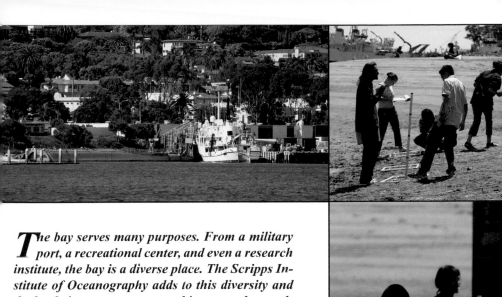

The bay serves many purposes. From a military port, a recreational center, and even a research institute, the bay is a diverse place. The Scripps Institute of Oceanography adds to this diversity and docks their many oceanographic research vessels in the bay. While Scripps looks at life deep in the ocean, we observe the life neighboring the facility.

to upgrade the scientific staff, buy a new oceanographic vessel, build an aquarium, and repair the sea wall. Vaughan was successful in laying the groundwork for many of these items, but was never able to fully fund all of them. Vaughan was frustrated at the University's lack of support and funding. Vaughan retired on September 1, 1936 and was succeeded by Harald Ulrik Sverdrup. (History of SIO" 2005)

Harald Ulrik Sverdrup, a Norwegian oceanographer and aretic scientist, accepted the position of director for only three years. Sverdrup focused on converting Scripps from a local institution to a world-renowned organization. He persuaded Robert Paine Scripps to purchase a new vessel capable of deep water exploration. The vessel named R/V E.Wh. Scripps conducted the first hydrographic survey of the Gulf of California. ("History of SIO" 2005)

In 1951, Roger Revelle became the fifth director. Revelle used his connections in Washington to gain federal funding for a fleet of research vessels. The Marine Physical Lab then began conducting extensive research in the Pacific. These expeditions led to a greater understanding of the oceans and the history of earth. ("History of SIO" 2005)

Edward Allan Frieman became director in 1986. Frieman was a big proponent for the theory of global warming. He conducted several experiments on the theory of climate change and advised the government about the topic. During Frieman's administration SIO acquired a new vessel, the R/V Roger Revelle, named after one of the Institute's most famous directors. Currently SIO at all its locations occupies sixty-seven buildings and 230 acres of land. They now operate four vessels that travel over 100,000 miles each year. ("History of SIO" 2005)

Uses

Some of the greatest discoveries in oceanography have come from scientists, support crew and the boats at the Scripps Nimitz facility. The facility sits on 5.7 acres of land in Point Loma. The 110 meter pier and 85 meter quay wall are home to five research ships and the platform FLIP. The R/V Roger Revelle, R/V Melville R/V New Horizon, R/V Robert Gordon Sproul and the Flip are the five largest and most famous Scripps research boats and are all parts of this facility. Each boat carries anywhere between two to eight scientists at any given point in time and provides them with facilities to perform independent or group research. Scientists and oceanographers choose an appropriate ship according to their destination, use of facilities and type of study. The most important part of the facility are the buildings adjacent to the pier, which include the control room of marine radio station WWD, scientific staging and storage areas, administrative offices, shipboard technical support spaces and offices. This large and equipped facility maintains, repairs, and modifies all the ships in order to keep them in outstanding condition and ready for various scientific expeditions. The storage room contains some of the most interesting research equipment in the world. Most of the equipment is hand-made by engineers and scientists for specific research purposes. Some of them are more generic and

are used to gather water samples, organisms, or bottom composition samples from the ocean. Scientific equipment is prepared, customized, loaded, unloaded and sent to scientists all over the world.

The R\V ships are some of the largest and most equipped ships of the facility. In the past forty years these boats have been a great contribution to science and oceanography. Named after the founder of UCSD, the R\V Roger Revelle was built in 1996. It is 273 feet long, has a 4,070 square foot deck and 4,000 square feet of lab spaces. It is one of the newest Scripps research boats. The 170 foot R/V New Horizon boat was built in 1978 and renovated in 1996. It was used to gather data regarding iron influence during upwelling events. In this experiment the ship was used to pull an undulating Towfish to gather salinity, optical, and temperature data. The R/V Melville is one of the older research ships. It was built in 1969 with 2,636 square feet of lab space. It has been on expeditions as far as the South China Sea. The R/V Robert Gordon Sproul was built in 1981 with wet, dry, and portable laboratories. The Sproul has been taking scientists around the world for the past twenty-four years. The Scripps research ships are available to oceanographers and scientists all around the world. All together they have steamed more than six million nautical miles in support of the academic and science community.

One cannot mention Scripps or their facility without elaborating on the astonishing Flip. The Flip is the most famous and advanced platform in the world. It is a phenomenon in engineering, physics, biology and oceanography. The idea of the Floating Instrument Platform (FLIP) was inspired by an observation of a floating broom that was extremely stable on the surface of water. The 355-foot long Flip was built in 1962. The platform is composed of a main galley that is attached to a 300-foot draft. It does not contain an engine so it's dragged out by other boats. While at shore the platform is in a horizontal position but when

dragged into the ocean the drift is filled with water causing an unbelievable 90 degree "flip" of the drift and galley. Since the draft is 300 feet under water the platform is extremely stable, easing the use of equipment and offering an opportunity for refined ocean measurements. In order to accommodate the 90 degree flip the galley hallways and rooms have two doors and special tables and chairs attached to the walls. While hard to believe, the revolutionary engineering of the platforms prevents a tea kettle from spilling during the forty-five-minute flipping processes.

This state-of-the-art platform was developed through the combined efforts of the Marine Physical Laboratory (MPL), Scripps Institution of Oceanography and the University of California, San Diego for the U.S. Navy. It was originally built for the U.S. Navy's SUBROC program and was used to measure effects of the environment on long-range sound propagation. Since then she has been used in the Atlantic and Pacific Ocean for a variety of research projects including meteorology, geophysics, physical oceanography, non-acoustic ASW and laser propagation experiments. But the projects are not what make her a phenomenon; it is her unique ability to flip into a vertical position and maintain a unique stable platform for researching oceanographers, biologists and scientists.

Another fascinating ship that belongs to the Scripps facility is the NOAA David Starr Jordan. The Ship was named after Dr. David Starr Jordan (1851-1931) who was one of the most famous and achieved educators and naturalists of his time. It was built in 1964 in Sturgeon Bay, Wisconsin by the U.S. Bureau of Commercial Fisheries which later became part of the National Oceanic and Atmospheric Administration. The ship was deployed to San Diego, California in 1996 in order to do fishery research in the tropical Pacific. The David Starr Jordan has traveled over a million miles in order to study the physical and biological oceanography of the southwestern U.S. coast and the eastern Pacific. Some of the most famous studies composed by the Starr Jordan include the Stenella Abundance

Research Project and a 3-year study on the status of dolphin stocks mistakenly captured by yellowfin tuna purse-seine fisheries in the eastern Pacific.

Location

Located on the shores of Point Loma, Marine Physical Laboratory (MPL) is surrounded by government facilities, public businesses, and private homes. The Marine Physical Laboratory of the Scripps Institution of Oceanography rests on the western side of the San Diego Bay. Shelter Island lies nearby on this western coast. Boat docks stretch along this side of the bay. Dozens of private backyards are interspersed with the boating facilities. There are no major stores or fast food chains at this far end of Point Loma. The beach near Marine Physical Laboratory is very enclosed and peaceful which makes it an ideal place for a family picnic or a secret hideaway for rest and relaxation. The directions to get to the Marine Physical Laboratory are simple. One can find it by going south on Rosecrans Street until it ends.

Sources

"History of SIO." Scripps Institution of Oceanography Archives. 5 May 2005. <http://scilib.ucsd.edu/sio/archives/siohstry/hist.html>.

Description and Feeling

Hidden from most, there is a little isolated beach down by Scripps Research Center. It is a safe haven for the locals to escape from their everyday lives and a place to center themselves in serenity. A cool breeze passes by, bringing with it a soft sense of comfort. The locals surround themselves with the calming sound of the crashing waves and the soothing beauty of the bay. The firm sand provides them with a comfortable walk to the bay and a soft ground to relax on. They feel safe, at home, and secure.

Yet, their sense of security fades away as we flock together and flow through the gates to their sacred beach. We come bearing food and a general lack of understanding for what the residents so greatly treasure. Though nervous, these locals are kind people who simply wait for us to leave. Much to their surprise, we are not the wild and rambunctious teenagers that television has led them to believe. They begin to feel comfortable with us around; one even lets us play with his dogs. Like clockwork, we all seem to glide away from the beach with ease; for it is time to retire to our buses for the day. The locals have control again. Everything is as it should be.

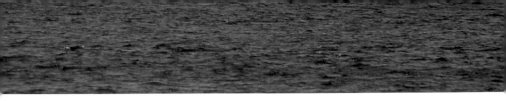

The Vagabond

The Vagabond set sail today
To where I don't really know
To far off places, or ones near by
Oh how I wish I, too, could go

I, too, long to see what the Sea Gypsies see
To spend days and nights out on the oceans
To let the wind be my guide and the water my life
Such things are truly beautiful notions

The Vagabond set sail today
I don't know when it is to return
But when it does I hope to hear
Of all the wonderful things it did learn

—Chandler Garbell

Biogeography

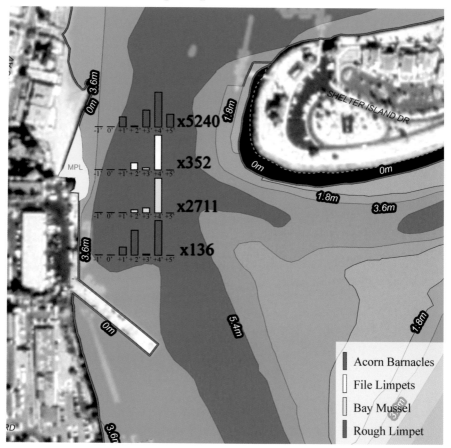

The above map displays a portion of the Marine Physical Lab where the biodiversity survey was conducted. The area in yellow is the approximate extent of the survey transects. The flat bar graphs on the image above represent the abundance of the four most common species arranged by tide heights. The bar on the far left is the abundance of creatures at a -1 foot tide height while the bar on the far right is the abundance at a +5 foot tide height. The highest count per creature was set as the 100% mark and the other bars were scaled to match that. As a result, the graphs are not proportionate to each other. A scale factor is immediately to the right of the graph. For example, a scale of x227 means that the maximum value is 227 times larger than a set constant.

Tide Height and Species Distribution at The Marine Physical Lab

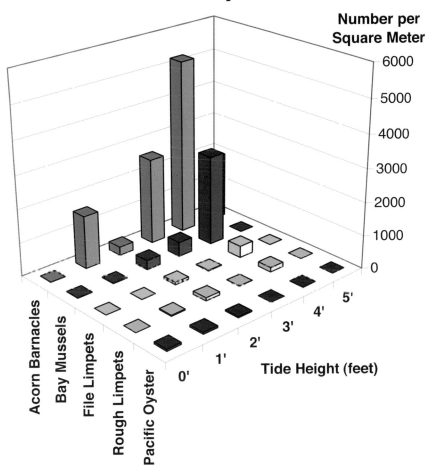

The above 3D graph represents the abundance of a certain species at a certain tide height. Just north of the Nimitz, Scripps Institute was an extremely abundant and biodiverse area. Notice the vertical scale compared to the other graphs and it becomes readily apparent of the extremely large numbers of creatures. While predominantly barnacles and mussels, this site had the highest concentration overall of any site.

CORONADO ISLAND

History of Coronado

The outer contour of the San Diego Bay is defined by Coronado Island. Coronado Island is actually a large, man-made peninsula that is connected by a narrow strand of land to the mainland far to the south in Imperial Beach. Coronado Island received its name from the Spanish explorer Sebastian Vizcaino, who chose to name it "Las Yslas Coronadas." The name stuck and was later translated into Coronado Island. In 1886, Coronado was bought for $110,000 by the Coronado Beach Company, which began to develop it as a commercial resort. Later that same year, the Coronado Ferry Company was formed and began to ferry the stream of tourists from downtown San Diego to the northeastern shores of Coronado. Over the years, the Coronado Beach Company turned the island into a resort town which included the groundbreaking of the now world-famous Hotel del Coronado on

We explore and reflect upon the shores of Coronado near the ever-popular ferry landing and Tidelands Park. As the eye travels the magnificent view of the San Diego skyline, the awe-inspiring Coronado Bridge rises from the shore. Yet even amongst the rock walls of the coast, we can find diverse and almost alien-looking intertidal creatures.

March 1887. The region's popularity soared, and as it did, boating clubs, schools, and residential communities quickly formed on the island, all within five years of Coranado's initial purchase by the Coronado Beach Company. ("History of Coronado" 2005)

In 1917 the military bought the North Island Air Station, located at the opening of the San Diego Bay. The military was particularly pleased with the area because the northern part of the island was in optimal condition for an airbase. As the military presence in San Diego grew, North Island and the rest of Coronado were filled in and built up with residences and businesses to resemble the shape it is today. ("Coronado California" 2005)

As the population of Coronado grew, residents and tourists became tired of taking one of five ferries to and from the island. This changed in February of

1969, as construction began on the San Diego Coronado Bridge which would eventually link the eastern end of the island to the city of San Diego. Six months later, the bridge became an icon of San Diego, spanning 2.12 miles and rising 200 feet above the waters of the San Diego Bay. Today the earthquake-proof, five-lane freeway carries over 70,000 vehicles a day and is tall enough to allow an aircraft carrier to pass underneath. ("Ruelas" 1999)

Uses

Coronado Island is currently a premier tourist attraction and military base. Hotel del Coronado and the surrounding beaches draw thousands of tourists, and the North Island Base can dock up to three aircraft carriers. The hotels and beaches on the side of the island facing towards the Pacific Ocean are some of the best in the city; the beaches span the entire western edge of the peninsula. The bay side of Coronado is most famous for the Coronado Bridge and the ferry landing. Thousands of people still take the 15-minute ferry ride to Coronado for its restaurants and the magnificent view of the San Diego skyline.

Location

Coronado Island is located at 32 degrees 40' North, and 117 degrees 10' West. The city is 7.7 square miles of land with a population of approximately 25,000 permanent residents. The falsely named island is actually a peninsula that is connected to the rest of San Diego by a narrow strip of land called the Silver Strand, which runs south from the island's eastern edge. Coronado was separated from North Island by a shallow channel called the Spanish Bight. When the Navy bought and developed its airbase on

North Island, they filled in the gap and joined the remaining regions to turn Coronado into one cohesive "island." The peninsula today stretches as far north as downtown and the San Diego airport, all the way down south to San Ysidro where the strand connects to the San Diego mainland. Beaches line the oceanic side of Coronado, while the interior bay coastline of Coronado includes Navy installations, commercial industries, and recreational marinas. ("The Origins of Coronado" 2005)

Sources:

"Coronado, California." Wikipedia. Mar. 2005. <http://en.wikipedia.org/wiki/Coronado,_California>.

Heart On A Pendulum

*There is a different point of view
at every turn, at every move.
The scene changes all the time.
To get it exact is impossible
when the world and mind
do not stay still.
Time does not freeze
the mind does not stop racing,
the heart does not stop pumping,
and eyes can't stop looking.
Here comes a boat, a bird, a person.
Their presence changes everything.
Include them in or exclude them out?
From the scene I choose pieces to make an image.
Shall it stay the same, or change gradually,
As time passes by my eyes?
The moving waves, the passing cars,
even rocks and structures change hues
as the day changes the world's appearance.
Change brings new experiences:
Physically, only slight changes come;
Mentally, well, the mind is more difficult to control.
Thoughts are hidden from view
The heart swings on a pendulum.*

-Christina Hernandez

"History of Coronado." Coronado Historical Association. May 2005.
<http://www.ecoronado.com/history.shtml>.

Ruelas, Ramon. San Diego - Coronado Bridge. 26 Feb. 1999.
<http://www.dot.ca.gov/hq/esc/tollbridge/Coronado/Corofacts.html>

The Origins of Coronado. Glorietta Bay Inn. July 1998.
<http://www.gloriettabayinn.com/coronado-history.html>

Description and Feeling

As I sit overlooking the bay, I slowly come to the realization that the bay and I are very similar. Today my mood reflects the weather; it is a particularly gray day, with no sun to brighten my spirit. The rocks bordering the shore are my body, ready to weather any storm. I am unsettled, much like the water, which is tumultuous and churning. The wind swirls, mirroring the emotions running through me. I feel uneasy, like there is a task that has been left unfinished, or something on the horizon that I have not anticipated. The clusters of trees are my friends and

family, who stand proudly and are always ready to support my endeavors. They are the buffer against the skyscrapers, reassurance that I will make it through. The city skyscrapers are the future events still to come. From across the bay they don't seem threatening, but up close, they are menacing. One of the smaller ones could be taking the SAT. The next biggest is graduation next year. The biggest of all may be going to college. The others are unpredictable, and their size undetermined, but they are as important as the rest. The construction on the far shore is the part of me that is still growing, still learning. Every once in a while, a boat floats by, like an opportunity I can't pass up. Each characteristic is unique to the bay. No other will ever look just like this. The bay is its own person, separate and individual from any other, just like me.

Escape To Freedom

Waves

Beat Down

Against My Consciousness

This Is God's Intent

This Life Tranquil Without Control

Did He Mean to Restrict Us?

But With Other's Influence We Hold Back

And The Human Nature Creates Its Own God

A God of Self Imposed Hate from Inside

Creating Tension We All Feel Yet Strive to Escape

Once Free We Can Do Anything Our Minds Can See

—Kevin Strong

Ballad of the Dead Seagull

Tick tock tick tock
How fun the Bay can be
From big fat crabs
To oyster halves
A sea anemone.

Oh to behold
I see I see
A seagull I do see
A closer look
Reveals to me
He's dead as dead can be.

Decay decay
Here at the Bay
The putrid smell of rot
A twisted wing
Raw flesh showing
The seagull must have fought.

Or maybe not or maybe not
Maybe he ate some trash
Eating the junk
Filled veins with gunk
Blood clots made the full crash

All that begins all that begins
Must end, it's only fair
But when it ends
Oh that depends
On how much one takes care

Tick tock tick tock
Time is up for the gull
The bay lives on
But when it's gone
Depends on how we live.

--Alexander N. Chee

Biology of Coronado

Many creatures live on Coronado Island apart from humans. While observing the animals of the intertidal zones, two types of animals stood out to be a recurring theme at the survey sights around the island. A type of diving bird called the tern and the many sea anemones in the intertidal surf were both signs of Coronado.

Terns

There are many types of terns that have been seen across the bay, but by far the most plentiful area was the time that we went to Coronado. In general, terns are interesting birds; they are usually considered similar and related to the gull; however, that is where the similarities end. They have a more streamlined body, a forked tail, and can hover and dive to catch their food. While the tern is seen worldwide, there are only 11 varieties that inhabit the west. Only 3 have we seen in our studies; those being the elegant, Fosters, and least tern. Terns are interesting creatures themselves; they are typically very long-flying birds, and can travel intercontinentally. They are typically sized around the same as a gull. They have long tails and very narrow wings, and hardly ever glide. They seem to be always beating their wings furiously in the air, hovering before diving down to come up with small fish or invertebrates. Except for their feeding, these birds do not usually enter the water, despite having webbed feet.

The elegant tern is not a typical San Diego resident. Until recently, it was victim to a declining population. Then El Niño came though. Since then it has had ever increasing numbers—numbers that are still rising. They seem to enjoy nesting on islands, and are 16-17 inches in length when fully grown. As with most terns the sexes appear the same. They can be easily distinguished from the Fosters tern by the presence of a black tip on the beak.

The Fosters tern is considered to be much like the common tern. It is a lighter variety and has a black cap and one of the most deeply forked

tails of all the terns. They are 14-15 inches in length and are partially character-ized by their nests, typically woven out of grass and lined with finer varieties of softer grass. The birds are small, slim and very quick, though can be easily sepa-rated from the Least Tern on size alone.

The Least Tern is the smallest member or the tern family at only 8.5 inches in length; they are tiny in comparison. They are also endangered, as their habitats are constantly being destroyed by humans. The California Least Tern, which is common in San Diego, was the first animal on the endangered animals list as of the 70's. It is easily recognized from other terns by their low flying and virtually invisible wing beat. With a blink of an eye, you can miss them entering the water, and never see the bird again.

Sea Anemones

Throughout our several adventures to the various bays of San Diego, we discov-ered many new and exciting species. However, the most unique species were found at the Ferry Landing on Coronado Island. There are four species of Antho-pleura, three of which occur locally in San Diego: elegantissima, sola, and arte-misia. *Anthopleura elegantissima*, better known as the Aggregating Anemone, is the most commonly found in rocky areas. *Anthopleura sola*, the large solitary one in shallow tide pools with stripes on its oral disk. *Anthopleura artemisia*, which is a solitary one that lives in bays and sandy areas; it burrows itself into the sand and is not seen often at low tide. People often forget that it exists. The anemone that is not here is *Anthopleura xanthogrammica*, also known as the Giant Green, which is found in colder water.

At Coronado we found A. elegantissima and A. artemisia. We have dis-cussed with Professor Paul Dayton, an oceanographer at the Scripps Institution of Oceanography, our ideas as to what limits their distribution. We believed that due to the lack of fine silt, the coarse sand does not shade them from the sun suf-ficiently. However, Professor Dayton replied that they can survive in coarse sand. Since we discovered them at the narrowest part of the bay, it is a possibility that the abundance of the water flow provides more food. This is an interesting idea because A. elegantissima tend to be filter feeders, but Professor Dayton suspects that they have enough food but also doubts his conclusion and advised that we test our idea by retrieving anemones onto plates so we can transplant them. We also feel that their location might have something to do with the difference in the water temperature. In Professor Dayton's experience, the bay water temperatures might actually be on the high end of what the anemones can handle. He left us with two other thoughts; the sedimentation of fine silts could hurt them and the bay is disturbed enough to have killed them in the few natural habitats they had. We all agree that anemones cannot recolonize their habitats very well. Therefore,

Professor Dayton believes it might be a historical mortality that we cannot know about due to their poor colonization ability.

In a study of artificial armored shorelines, also known as "riprap," that cover 74% of the San Diego bay, reports were given of sea anemones being sited at Embarcadero Park and Harbor Island. In November of 2000, J.L.D. Davis, L.A. Levin, and S.M. Walther from the Integrative Oceanography Division at the Scripps Institution of Oceanography observed that species richness was generally higher in exposed sites in the intertidal zone in November when the sea level was

higher, as opposed to in June and in protected sites. The richness decreased with the increasing distance from the bay mouth at the exposed sites. Anemones of the genus Anthopleura had the highest cover in the middle of San Diego Bay. Davis, Levin, and Walther did not observe the shores of Coronado Island, which is across from the Embarcadero Park and south from Harbor Island. By the sea anemone being found in the other two locations, our idea of the anemone being located at the narrowest part is supported. The middle of the bay is the narrowest part of the bay, which has a stronger water flow which means more food flow. We all agree that since A. elegantissima tend to be filter feeders, perhaps this is why they flourish in this location of the bay.

Biogeography

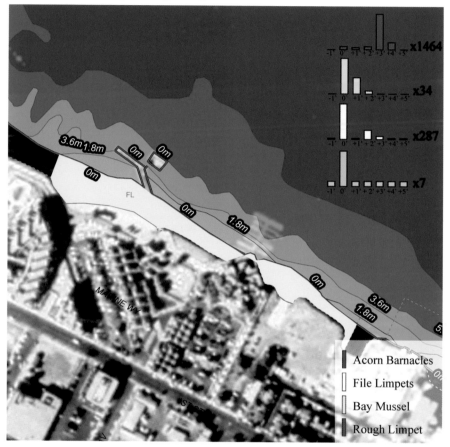

The above map displays a portion of the Coronado Ferry Landing where the bio-diversity survey was conducted. The area in yellow is the approximate extent of the survey transects. The flat bar graphs on the image above represent the abundance of the four most common species arranged by tide heights. The bar on the far left is the abundance of creatures at a -1 foot tide height while the bar on the far right is the abundance at a +5 foot tide height. The highest count per creature was set as the 100% mark and the other bars were scaled to match that. As a result, the graphs are not proportionate to each other. A scale factor is immediately to the right of the graph. For example, a scale of x227 means that the maximum value is 227 times larger than a set constant.

Tide Height and Species Distribution at The Coronado Ferry Landing

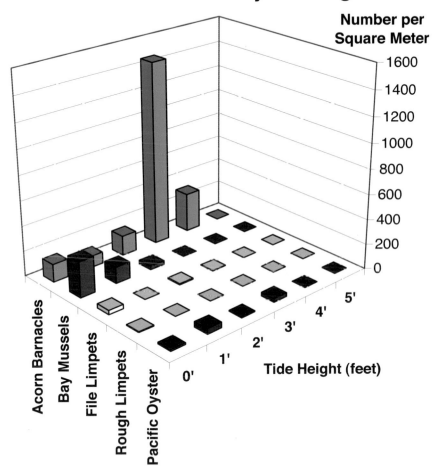

The above 3D graph represents the abundance of a certain species at a certain tide height. The first site on Coronado Island was near the Ferry Landing. Apart from the sudden barnacle spike at +3 foot tide height, this site had a large number of creatures at relatively low tides around +0 and +1 feet. Nearly all the higher tidal levels were devoid of biodiverse life.

Biogeography

The above map displays a portion of Tidelands Park where the biodiversity survey was conducted. The area in yellow is the approximate extent of the survey transects. The flat bar graphs on the image above represent the abundance of the four most common species arranged by tide heights. The bar on the far left is the abundance of creatures at a -1 foot tide height while the bar on the far right is the abundance at a +5 foot tide height. The highest count per creature was set as the 100% mark and the other bars were scaled to match that. As a result, the graphs are not proportionate to each other. A scale factor is immediately to the right of the graph. For example, a scale of x227 means that the maximum value is 227 times larger than a set constant.

Tide Height and Species Distribution at Tidelands Park

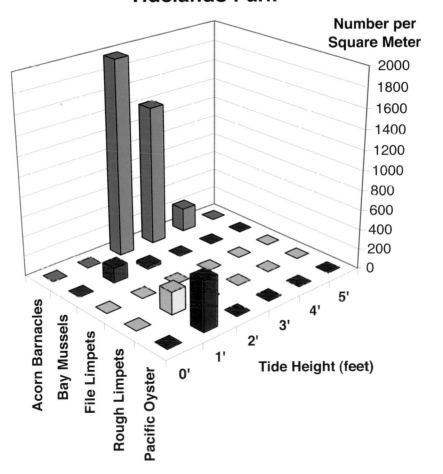

The above 3D graph represents the abundance of a certain species at a certain tide height. This area was unique in the fact that the shore had a very shallow slope and large portions of land were uncovered when the tides recessed. This can be partially seen in the GIS map on the preceding page. This may explain the clustering of creatures around the +2 and +3 tide heights. These heights did not see a lot of horizontal water movement because the slope was much steeper there. Once again this was one of the most abundant and biodiverse sites in the Bay.

Summative
Analysis
of the San Diego Bay

The Aspects of the Bay
in Its Entirety

*N*ow that all aspects around the bay have been explored, one must look at the bay as a whole to truly grasp its nature. When the broader picture is observed, one can see the implications and connections that San Diego has with its Bay. How this connection affects the life within the bay is one of the main focuses of this guide. The true scope of biodiversity within the bay can not be grasped until it is observed as a whole throughout the bay. The goal of this chapter is to analyze and quantify the distribution and biodiversity of intertidal creatures throughout the bay. As the results of this study are announced, the next step is to analyze the larger reasons behind these results. This leads to inquiry of the relationship between the human city of San Diego, and the civilization of natural intertidal life.

BIODIVERSITY ANALYSIS

One of the main purposes of this guide was to assess the biodiversity of common intertidal creatures around San Diego bay in hopes of drawing conclusions based upon our findings. In order to determine biodiversity, the creatures had to be surveyed and counted at various locations scattered throughout the bay. The presence of certain creatures and their numbers at certain tide heights can, when compared on multiple factors, give indications on features such as the natural health of the bay. The exact procedures of this study were discussed in the Biodiversity and Biogeography chapter of this book.

In order to present meaningful data to the reader, five of the most common intertidal creatures were selected to display results.

Acorn Barnacle

Bay Mussel

File Limpet

Rough Limpet

Pacific Oyster

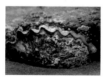

There were 9 survey sites at 6 different locations. One was at the Marine Physical Lab at the Nimitz Scripps Institute; another two at Point Loma Seafood and a site further in the America's Cup Harbor. There were two sites at the tip of shelter island. Shelter Island West was on the northwestern site of the island facing the harbor while Bali Hai was on the northeastern side of the island facing the bay right next to the Bali Hai restaurant. Another site was at the Spanish Landing underneath the Harbor Drive bridge at the mouth of the boat channel. The following site was at the northern end of the boat channel located just west of the San Diego International Airport. The final two sites were on Coronado Island. One was near the ferry landing and the other was at Tidelands park near the Coronado bridge.

Average Creature Count Per Species Per Location

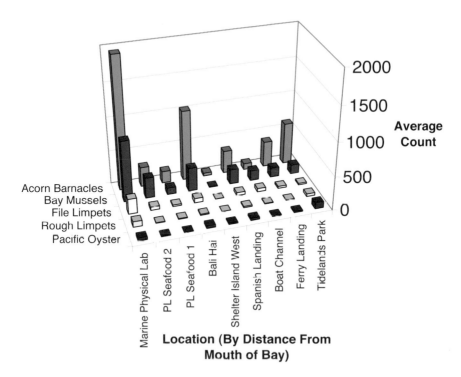

The above graph shows the average species abundance at a certain location for a certain species. On the bottom on the x-axis are the different survey sites arranged from closest to the mouth of San Diego bay to the furthest into the bay. Going in on the z-axis are the 5 common species that were used to assess the bay. Going up and down on the y-axis is the average number of creatures found for the particular site and species.

The most average abundant species and site are the Acorn Barnacles at the Marine Physical Lab at the Scripps Institute. As the locations become further away from the mouth of the bay, it appears that the average count decreases slightly; however, the data is very sporadic with extreme highs and extreme lows next to each other.

Average Creature Count Per Species Per Location (Bay Exposure Graph)

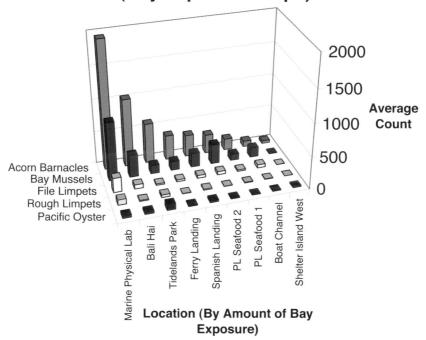

Location (By Amount of Bay Exposure)

The above graph shows the average species abundance at a certain location for a certain species. On the bottom on the x-axis are the different survey sites arranged on two factors. The primary is the amount of average exposure to the bay while the secondary is the distance from the mouth of the bay. The other axes are the same as they were in the previous graph.

This graph shows a direct correlation of the amount of bay exposure with the average number of creatures living in the location. The furthest left bars represent data taken at the Marine Physical Lab. This location is on a beach that is not hindered by any sort of harbor or breakwater. Similar conditions are found at Bali Hai and Tidelands Park. The Ferry Landing and the Spanish Landing both are somewhat sheltered by piers and man made islands. Both Point Loma Seafood sites, the Boat Channel, and the western side of Shelter Island are encased inside of harbors or inlets with extremely little direct Bay exposure.

ANALYSIS OF ABUNDANCE PER SPECIES

Acorn Barnacle

The graph below shows the abundance for the acorn barnacle across various sites and at increasing heights above the mean 0 foot tide. It is most abundant at the +4' tide height and at the Marine Physical Lab.

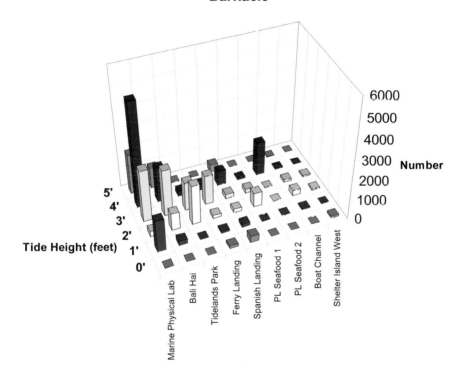

Tide Height and Abundance Across San Diego Bay for Acorn Barnacle

Bay Mussel

While the barnacles may have the most in numbers, the bay mussel has the greatest biodiversity. The unusual aspect about this data is the noticeable shift towards the right of the graph of the data which represents less exposure to the bay. It seems that the mussels can survive and flourish in locations around +1 foot tide height in harsher conditions.

Tide Height and Abundance Across San Diego Bay for Bay Mussel

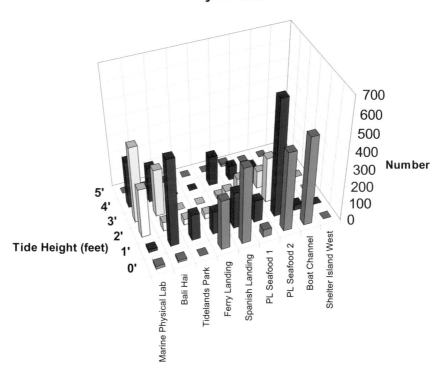

File Limpet

A large number of file limpets were found 4 feet above mean 0 ft tide at the Marine Physical Lab. Apart from that location, the distribution seems to be relatively random with a few spikes around the tide heights of 2, 3, and 4 foot. This may indicate that the file limpet does not need large quantities of water in order to survive, but can live in many different conditions.

Tide Height and Abundance Across San Diego Bay for File Limpet

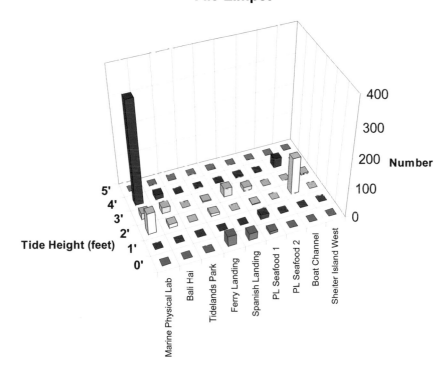

Rough Limpet

Large quantities of rough limpets were found in Tidelands Park at the +1 foot tide height. Strangely enough, the very few of the similar file limpet were found at this location and tide height. The random nature of the data suggests that like the file limpet, this creature survives in a variety of conditions and is very tolerable to the amount of water exposure it receives.

Tide Height and Abundance Across San Diego Bay for Rough Limpet

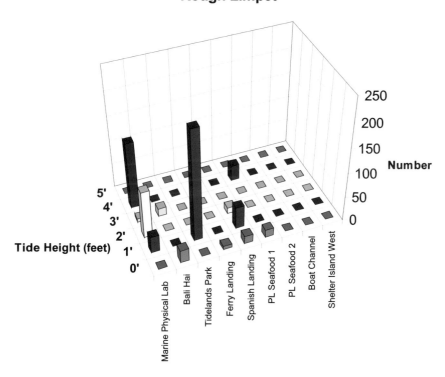

Pacific Oyster

The oyster was primarily found in lower tide heights such as +0', +1', and +2' tide heights. This indicates that the oyster needs to be covered by water often to survive. The extreme lack of data for the higher tide heights also indicates that oysters are not very tolerant of water level changes and require the constant flow of the ocean for food and air.

Tide Height and Abundance Across San Diego Bay for Pacific Oyster

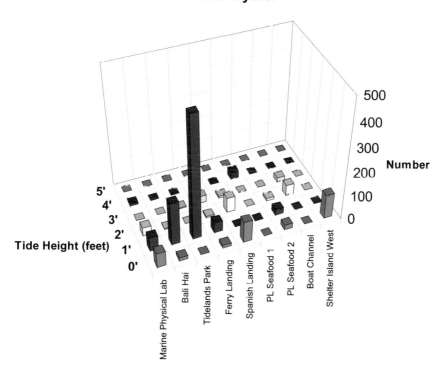

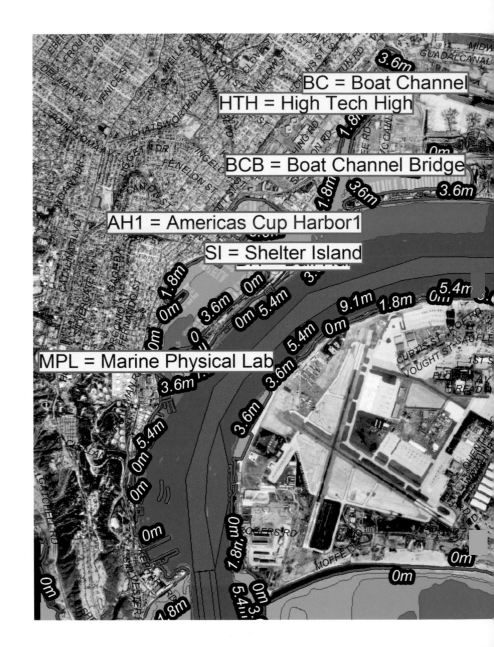

BC = Boat Channel
HTH = High Tech High
BCB = Boat Channel Bridge
AH1 = Americas Cup Harbor1
SI = Shelter Island
MPL = Marine Physical Lab

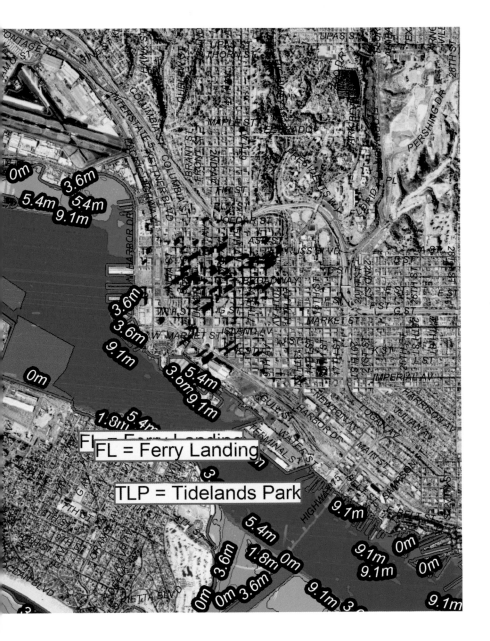

FL = Ferry Landing

TLP = Tidelands Park

BIODIVERSITY MATRIX

Species / Location:	Boat Channel	Bali Hai	Shelter Island West	Point Loma Seafood 1
Acorn Barnacle	X	X	X	X
Bay Mussel	X	X		X
File Limpet	X	X	X	X
Rough Limpet		X		X
Pacific Oyster	X	X	X	X
Gray Periwinkle	X	X		X
Bubble Snail				X
Serpulorbis	X	X		
Slipper snail				
Shore Crab	X	X		X
Rock Louse				X
Tunicate		X		X
Sponge	X			
Byrozoan	X			
Sea anemone (lg. solitary)				
Sea anemone (sm. colonial)				

   This table is a checklist of creatures found at different sites. The rows
are the 16 most common intertidal species while the columns represent the
different sties around the bay. An "X" means that a particular specimen was
found at that particular site. This document allows a reader to see which locations around the bay have a large amount of biodiversity. For example, the Ferry

Point Loma Seafood 2	Coronado: Tidelands Park	Coronado: Ferry Landing	Marine Physical Lab	Spanish Landing
X	X	X	X	X
X	X	X	X	
		X	X	
	X	X	X	
	X	X	X	X
X				
		X	X	
		X		
X	X	X	X	
			X	
		X	X	
		X		
	X			

Landing at Coronado Island has the highest biodiversity with 10 different species identified. Conversely, the Boat Channel Bridge near the Spanish Landing has only 2 types of identified species. This can also show which species are the most prevalent. For example, the Acorn Barnacle is present at all locations.

1 2 3 4 5 6 7 8 9 10 11 12 13 14 15 16 17 18 19 20 21 22 23 24 25 26

SPECIES KEY

Great Blue Heron: 1
Least Tern: 2
Osprey: 3
Pigeon: 4
Kingfisher: 5
Brown Gull: 6
Harbor Seal: 7
Bay Bass: 8
Brant: 9
Brown Pelican: 10
Bufflehead: 11
Crested Cormarant: 12
Malard: 13
Least Grebe: 14
Ruddy: 15
Redhead Duck: 16
Pintaill: 17
Greater Scaup: 18
Loon: 19
Brants Cormorant: 20
Red Shoulderd Hawk:21
Snowy Egret: 22
Barn Swalow: 23
Black Phoebe: 24
House Finch: 25
Western Grebe: 26

SAN DIEGO BAY BIO-DIVERSITY

Jared Diamond's Factors and the Future of the Environment

Over the spring semester, we were introduced to the work of Jared Diamond, author of *Guns, Germs, and Steel* and *Collapse*. Jared Diamond is a professor of physiology, geography, and environmental health at UCLA. Diamond is a foremost theorist of the evolution of civilizations and natural history. We read excerpts and reviews from *Collapse* and watched audio of professor Diamond's presentation at San Diego's Natural History Museum. Diamond discussed several factors which have led to civilizations' collapse: environmental damage, climate change, enemies, trading partner change, and social denial or elite isolation from the problem. In this paper, we will attempt to apply these factors to survey locations previously discussed in this Field Guide. The conclusions in this paper were given their support from vigorous intertidal surveys, our observations in the field, and assumptions we made back in the classroom. This application of Diamond's ideas is included here to provoke thought and speculation about the state of our environment and the consequences of human activity.

Spanish Landing – Climate Change and Trading Partners

The Spanish Landing is a little memorial to history where anyone who deems so can visit the seed of San Diego. It is a somewhat natural and quiet place in the middle of a hustling and bustling city. Given the tranquility of the place, it is hard to imagine any possibility of danger or collapse. If one looks out across the great Bay, a field of commerce in motion emerges. The San Diego Bay greets ships from all nations and of all stripes.

Spaniards first explored this place on a conquest to take California and inhabit it. At this time, there was no grand shipping entrance to the San Diego Bay; the channel at its deepest was fifteen feet. Since then, the Bay has been chiseled to fit the needs of military, travel cruise liners, and import ships. This dramatic change is not so evident to anyone who is not well acquainted with this place. But a look back at the maps before the arrival of the military and commercial shipping shows that this is no longer at all the same place.

Spanish Landing history gives the visitor a clue that changes might still occur here. If we apply Jared Diamond's principles, the issue of trading partner change becomes important. A change in the patterns of international trade could be devastating to San Diego's economy. Jared Diamond might question whether or not this place relies too highly on trade. We might question what factors might lead San Diego to lose such vital trading partners.

In a recent study by the Army Corps of Engineers, San Diego was tested for its susceptibility to a tsunami. A proportionate replica was made of the harbor and waves. San Diego does not have a continental shelf to diminish waves. In fact the only geographic wave barrier is a small sand spit called Silver Strand. The results of  the tests proved that most of the waves generated over-topped the lowly elevated Silver Strand and spilled into the inner harbor. Spanish Landing sits at the turn of San Diego Bay and represents the true heart of our city's maritime trade. If such a vital enterprise was overrun by a tsunami the results might be long-term devastation. Thus, two of Jared Diamond's factors, climate change and the loss of trade partners are brought to mind when Spanish Landing is considered.

America's Cup Harbor – Human Environmental Damage

America's Cup Harbor houses a popular restaurant known as Point Loma Seafood. The restaurant lies just a few yards from the shore, where fishing boats are in plain sight. Our class surveyed the polluted shore. We ate the seafood fresh

out of the nearby ocean. During this time we noticed a number of environmental issues.

The most obvious environmental issue at hand is overfishing. For thousands of years, humans have been fishing for food. However, it was only recently that fishing has become a mass industry that employs environmentally destructive methods to increase profits. The fishing industry, in its quest to meet the demand for seafood and maximize efficiency and profits, has had a significant negative effect on many species of fish, depleting populations and disturbing ecosystems. While these methods may provide plenty of food and money now, they are not sustainable in the long run. The effects of overfishing have already become apparent in many areas where communities depend on the harvest of fish for food. Fish, when harvested in an ecologically unsound manner, can become a non-renewable resource, which will harm not only the fish but the people that depend on them.

A quick glance across the shore next to Point Loma Seafood will reveal

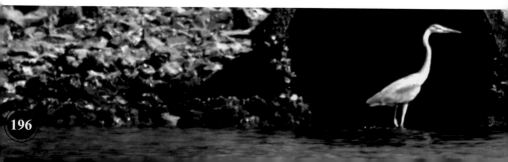

a number of sources of chemical pollution in the ocean. Pipes allow industrial waste and sewage water to flow into the bay. The boats also pollute the ocean in many ways, such as leaking oil, burning fuel, and paints. The combination of overfishing and pollution has done a great deal of damage to the marine habitat and the life around it.

When contemplating Jared Diamond's theory of societal collapse in the context of this particular location, human environmental damage is clearly the first factor that comes to mind. This industrial use of a natural habitat could lead to an ecological disaster. It is only a matter of time before these environmental hazards become a problem for humans, and this problem could escalate to contribute to societal collapse.

Shelter Island – Denial of the Problem

Shelter Island is familiar to many who seek a relaxing day, boating facilities, or a seafood restaurant. It is an abode to houseboats and weekend sailors who need a place to moor their ships. During work hours it is not hard to find tour buses, roller skaters, and people enjoying the view from their cars. In fact, Shelter Island's need for incoming sightseers that has made it vulnerable to one of Jared Diamond's five factors. That factor occurs when a community denies there is a problem to the environment in the first place.

While Shelter Island might not be a thriving civilization in the same order as those in *Collapse*, nonetheless, similarities and parallels exist. For instance, Shelter Island is so dependent on tourism that if such a resource were halted, the restaurants and hotels there would cease to exist. This is why those who make a living in this industry are so susceptible to denial of the problem. If the beachfront were to become so polluted that animals and other life were threatened, the reputation of the beach would suffer. Businesses would never admit to this, since distraught travelers would head to another location.

Shelter Island may not fit such a dire description, but in the future it may. The beach, the public accommodations, and the fresh seafood are essential to the Island's success. It is easy for the business community to let its guard down. It is much harder to provide the best care for the local environment. In order for this community to prosper in the future, it must immediately recognize and deal with environmental damage rather than deny such problems exist. The place can only survive if the people there respect the gift of the ocean and help preserve it for future business and livelihoods.

The Boat Channel – Threat of Enemies

The Boat Channel is part of the former Naval Training Center. The Naval Training Center produced a great deal of toxic industrial waste when it was a military base. Since then, most of the property has been sold for development and the Navy has abandoned much of the area. Unfortunately a proper environmental cleanup never took place. The Boat Channel is particularly hazardous, with dangerous amounts of zinc, lead, copper, and a banned pesticide called DDT. It has the highest heavy metal contamination in all of San Diego Bay. Even without prior knowledge of this, a trip to the Boat Channel will easily reveal its disgusting state upon viewing the clearly filthy water and smelling the repulsive fluids along the shore. The city and the Navy have been arguing about a cleanup, but it has yet to happen. The presence of these environmental toxins poses health risks for both the marine life and the surrounding human communities.

San Diego is historically a Navy town, and the Boat Channel is full of reminders of its military past; this city still has many military bases that are active. These days, the United States has become very militaristic. In its quest to fight the War on Terrorism, the United States has begun to make many new enemies. Americans seem to think that fighting more wars will increase our chances of survival in the long run.

However, worldwide anti-American sentiment is currently growing as a result of U.S. foreign policy and international military action. At this rate, regardless of how powerful it may be, the United States could eventually be subdued by an anti-American world majority. Ironically, by seeking to increase our "defense," the nation might be increasing our susceptibility to the threat of enemies. The United States might want to consider altering its foreign policy if it wishes to prevent enemies leading to its collapse.

Thus, the Boat Channel reminds observers of two of Jared Diamond's five factors: human environmental destruction and the threat of enemies. The military wreaked environmental havoc on this place years ago, and the problems haven't gone away. Also, the military presence reminds one of the nation's current trends of militarism, and the potential issues involving enemies.

Scripps Marine Physical Lab – Addressing Climate Change

One of the five factors leading to societal collapse mentioned by Jared Diamond is climate change. Throughout history, nature has gone through cycles of climate change, beyond the control of humans, which helped wipe out civilizations. We are currently in a global warming trend; however, this time it can be attributed to human activity. Countless scientific studies suggest that many of the gases emitted by industrialized nations create a greenhouse effect, trapping heat inside the Earth's atmosphere. The Marine Physical Laboratory, an academic lab of the Scripps Institution of Oceanography (SIO), studies many aspects of the ocean that are affected by climate change. It's hard to spend a day at the MPL without having the issue of global warming cross your mind.

Due to the relationship between temperature and the status of the ocean, Scripps's research naturally demonstrates the effects climate change has on the ocean. Some of their boats are used for scientific expeditions to study hurricanes and tsunamis, which are partially caused by changes in temperature. These natural disasters have the potential to do great amounts of damage, as is evidenced by the recent tsunami strike in Asia. Scientists at the SIO have also recently proved the link between human activity, greenhouse gases, and climate change. They have observed changes in the surface temperature of the ocean, and a series of computer models indicates that the effect is human-caused.

The ocean is just one place we are beginning to see the effects of climate change. Climate change

can have negative impacts on society in a number of other ways. Changes in temperature can affect crop yield, and thus the availability of food. Forest fires caused by intense heat can blaze thousands of acres of land, destroying many houses, which happened just recently in California. A disruption of normal temperatures will inevitably alter the water cycle in many areas, which could create a water crisis. If the polar ice caps melt, a large flood (or possible ice age) could wipe out millions of people. Thus the Marine Physical Lab has shown the human impact upon our climate. Jared Diamond has shown us that climate change has devastated societies throughout history, and the same could happen to us if we don't act soon.

Coronado Island – Elite Isolation

Coronado Island is a place that is not known for being polluted or dirty. The location differs from other environments on the San Diego Bay. Its beaches are home to numerous animals and it is a thriving place of business and tourism. The beaches are accessible and attract tourists to the Island. However, these beaches themselves are somewhat harder to get to than other beaches in San Diego. Coronado is accessible only on the ferry or over the Coronado Bay Bridge. If Jared

Diamond were to apply his factors onto Coronado, he might say the Island is effected by elite isolation. He might also conclude the Island is certainly dependent upon its military presence and, as a consequence, the threat of enemies.

A military presence is seen on Coronado Island, as the Island is split into two parts, one to the city of Coronado and the other half devoted to North Island Navy Air Station. Jared Diamond has hypothesized that an enemy could bring the demise of a civilization. When standing on the coast of Coronado it is easy to notice Coast Guard boats patrolling the waters with guns in hand. Maps reveal the military presence in San Diego surrounds and includes the City of

Coronado. Since the bombing of Pearl Harbor, San Diego, with Coronado at its center, has become the Navy's main Pacific Port. Does that make the city and the Island a target for those who want to make a stand against America? Perhaps not. But the economy of San Diego and much of Coronado is greatly dependent on the continued idea of war that may sooner or later occur.

Coronado Island can be named the jewel of San Diego. It lies in seclusion from the rest of San Diego. Using Jared Diamond's perspective, Coronado might be considered a classic case of elite isolation. This place is the home to many wealthy who live away from, or isolated from, the rest of San Diego. The Coronado Bridge is the only real connection between it and the rest of San Diego. What is the rest of San Diego like? Unlike Coronado, many houses in San Diego proper have bars on their windows. Many residents of San Diego are in fear of crime or gangs. Street improvements are behind schedule, and, aesthetically speaking, the city does not always inspire. People on the mainland of San Diego are just trying to support their families. It might be said that the residents of Coronado are worried about enjoying the finer things in life. One might ask if those on Coronado are in tune to the rest of San Diego and the struggles of the majority? To the extent that the people on Coronado are responsible for environmental policy and political decisions of areas beyond their Island, they may not be capable. A problem arises when rulers or leaders do not have an idea of conditions beyond their gates or borders. They may have no idea of how to adequately deal with the problem. They simply don't know what's going on. As Diamond has pointed out, such elite isolation can lead to collapse.

As we have discussed in this paper, the factors of environmental damage, climate change, enemies, trading partner change, and social denial or elitism all play a role in a civilization's demise. However, some more than others are the case of San Diego. Of these factors, the one most detrimental and likely to occur is our denial of the problem. It may not be at the hands of an enemy that we shall meet our collapse but by our own actions. If the public's attention is not brought to global warming and diminishing resources, not only will trading partners be lost but wars will be waged over such valued resources. This denial is further evident in that neither the Navy nor the city want to take responsibility for the cleanup of the Boat Channel. It is evident in the ceaseless production of leviathan SUVs. Jared Diamond refers to civilizations becoming desensitized to eminent and catastrophic problems. Are we staring blindly in the face of our own demise? Such mistakes have occurred in the past. If we study past civilizations that have fallen and identify parallel issues that occur today, we may learn from our mistakes, and make for ourselves a better life today and better future tomorrow. -- *John Horn & Will Gomez-Hicks*

References

"A Model Study of Wave Run-up at San Diego, California." Vicksburg, Mississippi: R. W. Whalin, 1969.

Aguilera, Mario, and Cindy Clark. "Scripps Researchers Find Clear Evidence of Human-Produced Warming in World's Oceans." Scripps Institution of Oceanography. 17 Feb. 2005. 24 May 2005. <http://scrippsnews.ucsd.edu/article_detail.cfm?article_num=666>.

Diamond, Jared. *Collapse*. New York.: W. W. Norton & Company , 1999.

Diamond, Jared . *Guns, Germs, and Steel: The Fates of Human Societies*. New York.: Reed Business Information, Inc., 1999. 0-480.

"Toxic Concerns: Naval Training Center (NTC) San Diego." Save Our NTC, Inc, San Diego. 24 May 2005. <http://www.ntcsd.org/about.html>.

Environmental Stewards of the Bay, and How You Can Become One

San Diego Bay is a delicate natural habitat facing numerous threats to its health and that of its inhabitants. Numerous non-profit organizations are currently acting as environmental stewards of the Bay. The authors of this field guide would like to encourage community involvement in the local conservation movement through participation in the activities of these organizations. The following organizations work specifically for San Diego Bay: Aquatic Adventures, Chula Vista Nature Center, Friends of Famosa Slough, Pro Peninsula, San Diego Audubon Society, Environmental Health Coalition, Surfrider Foundation, Wild Coast, Southwest Wetlands Interpretive Association, and San Diego Baykeeper. These unique organizations each have a range of volunteer opportunities for you to get involved in. There are also lots of ways you can work to reduce the burden you place on San Diego Bay. Through cooperation with these organizations and adopting an eco-friendly lifestyle, we can make a great difference in the well-being of the Bay.

   Aquatic Adventures works to provide educational programs to teach youth about marine science, expose them to marine habitats, and inspire environmental stewardship. The organization targets students that are traditionally underprivileged when it comes to science and technology, empowering them with the resources and opportunities to achieve their full potential and make a difference in the world. They have set up a Living Laboratory, where Summer Camps are held to teach students about marine biology and allow

them to interact with marine organisms. Volunteer opportunities range from classroom instruction to fieldwork. The teaching positions allow you to teach students about marine science in elementary schools, middle schools, high schools, and summer camps. You may contribute your time and labor to Friends of San Diego River Mouth as well, assisting them to preserve and restore the wetland and upland habitats in the areas where the Pacific Ocean meets the San Diego River. Aquatic Adventures also holds an annual community event called Wetland Avengers, where volunteers have joined forces to restore fragile salt marsh and sand dune habitats. If you are interested in volunteering with Aquatic Adventures, visit their website at http://www.aquaticadventures.com.

    The Chula Vista Nature Center is an internationally recognized aquarium/zoo, a living museum, which showcases many of the flora and fauna native to San Diego Bay and local wetland habitats. Their goal is to expose the public to the natural side of the bay's unique habitat and to promote environmental stewardship through education. Their living exhibits include eagles, shorebirds, hawks, sharks, stingrays, and jellyfish. The nature center also offers in-school and field trip programs to educate students about coastal resource conservation. Volunteer opportunities amount to a wide range of tasks needed to operate the facility; positions include interpretive guides (teachers), bird and nature walk leaders, aquarium crew, gift shop crew, bird crew, reptile crew, office assistants, newsletter crew, garden crew, nature crafts, board members, and maintenance crew. For more information about the nature center and volunteer opportunities, visit the CVNC website at http://www.chulavistanaturecenter.org.

    Friends of Famosa Slough is a non-profit corporation comprised of concerned citizens that work to preserve the natural habitat of Famosa Slough, a 37-acre wetland between Ocean Beach and the San Diego Sports Arena. They arrange cleanups, nature walks, and are involved in restoration projects. They also serve as a community voice and source of information regarding the slough. The organization offers teachers the opportunity to use the slough to as a hands-on resource to teach wetlands ecology, but conducts its own education projects, instructing students in classrooms, training students to monitor water quality, and mentoring students working on science fair projects. There are many volunteer opportunities available to get involved in fieldwork, education projects, and public outreach. Fieldwork positions include removing non-native plants, erosion control, trail maintenance, nurturing native plants, and monitoring water quality. You can also assist in classroom presentations, guided field trips,

or public events such as EarthFair. Visit the Friends of Famosa Slough website at http://www.famosaslough.org/ for more info.

Pro Peninsula is a bi-national non-profit organization that works on both sides of the US-Mexico border, with a focus on the protection of the natural environment of the Baja California peninsula. They are located in San Diego, and they have produced a number of projects that target San Diego Bay. Examples of these projects include beach cleanups and in-school and field trip programs on sea turtle conservation. Ongoing volunteer opportunities range from representing Pro Peninsula at informational booths, office help, event planning, assisting with environmental education, assisting in beach cleanups, and material development. More information is accessible at http://www.propeninsula.org/.

The San Diego Audubon Society is the local chapter of a national organization that fosters the protection of birds and other wildlife and advocates environmental conservation. Their projects constitute lobbying to prevent development that damages wildlife, spreading awareness about issues such as the depletion of the Salton Sea, maintaining the Silverwood Wildlife Sanctuary, organizing bird-watching field trips, and counting and monitoring wildlife around San Diego. Normal volunteer possibilities number among manning tables at events, participating in cleanup and habitat restoration projects, hosting guests and maintaining trails/habitats at the Silverwood Wildlife Sanctuary, counting birds, leading nature hikes, classroom presentations, spreading awareness about environmental issues, helping out at the SD Audubon office, or filling a position in one of various committees that run the organization. The SD Audubon Society is beginning a new project to help restore the San Diego River, which will entail a great deal of field labor, monitoring of the wildlife and its environment, educational projects, outreach, and environmental advocacy. The project needs many volunteers, and you can make a great difference by getting involved. An

abundance of information is available at their website, http://www.sandiegoaudubon.org/.

San Diego Baykeeper is a non-profit organization dedicated to preserving the bays, watersheds, and coastal waters of San Diego, California. Activities include arranging beach cleanups, organizing community events and environmental fairs such as Save the Bay 2005, educating students about the marine environment and its threats, managing a Harbor Safety Committee, monitoring and restoring kelp, and monitoring the quality of water in the bay. SD Baykeeper is looking for volunteers to fill the following positions: monitoring water and pollution, conducting policy research, maintaining boats, entering data, designing graphics, printing newsletters, cleaning beaches, and planning events. San Diego Baykeeper also encourages people to take it upon themselves to look out for ocean polluters and report suspicious activity. The SD Baykeeper website provides a wealth of information, and can be reached at http://www.sdbaykeeper.org/.

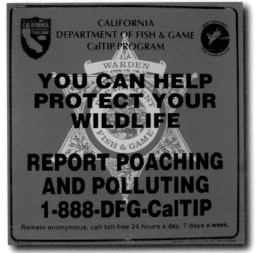

Many of us are contributing to the destruction of the bay without even realizing it. There are many things you can personally do to reduce pollution in San Diego Bay. Your home may be a source of toxic substances entering the ocean. Make sure you recycle your recyclable home waste, such as paper, plastic, and glass. When available, try to use non-toxic household products. Absorb your hazardous spills with kitty litter. Used toxic waste and household products can be safely disposed at a Hazardous Waste Facility. Pet waste contains bacteria that can be harmful if released into the bay. When walking with your pets, carry a plastic bag in case they need to defecate. Dispose of their waste in the trash or the toilet. Cars can release a number of substances harmful to the environment, such as gas, oil, auto fluids, and soaps. Try to use your car less often by carpooling and taking public transportation when possible, and riding your bike or walking for short distance trips. Keep your car in good repair, and, if neces-

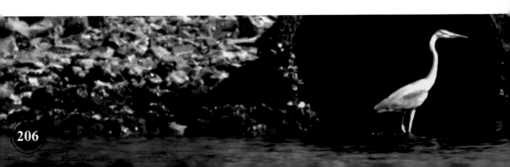

sary, use rags or pans to prevent leaks. Take your car to a car wash that recycles water. If you must wash your car at home, use water and cleaners sparingly, and use biodegradable cleaners if possible. A shutoff nozzle on your hose will help you conserve water. Used anti-freeze and motor oil can be recycled (free guide available by calling 858-467-0903). Streets and sidewalks act as outlets for trash and other waste to enter the ocean. If you see dirt, leaves or trash on the sidewalk, driveway, or patio, sweep it up rather than hosing it into the street. Instead of littering, dispose of trash in the proper containers. Refrain from dumping waste into streets and storm drains. If you have the option, choose planting over paving, as plants can help absorb runoff. The way you choose to nurture and protect your yard can have serious impacts on the environment. Avoid pesticide use by using beneficial insects and insecticidal soaps to control pests. Fertilize your plants with compost, rather than synthetic fertilizers. If rain is forecasted, hold off on the pesticides and fertilizers. Do not over-water your lawn, and it is better to follow a frequent, yet less intensive watering procedure, preferably during cooler times of the day. Furnish your garden with drought-resistant and native plants when possible. Native plants do not typically require any fertilizer or pesticides, and they require very little water after their first year. By making an effort to take up some of these eco-friendly habits, you will be drastically reducing your negative impact on San Diego Bay.

Take action: active and influential conservation organizations are needed to preserve the ocean habitat of San Diego Bay. They are currently doing wonderful work, but they still desperately need your help to combat the constant threats to this delicate environment. Monetary donations are always appreciated, but what better way to show your commitment to the local conservation movement than to participate in the projects put forth by these organizations. You have a wide assortment of ways to contribute, and a myriad of ways to apply countless skills. The non-profit world relies on volunteers to succeed, and you can certainly make a difference in the health of San Diego Bay by getting involved.

Health of the Bay Subcommittee:
San Diego Bay Advisory Committee for Ecological Assessment

In recent years, initiatives to clean the San Diego Bay have become entrapped in the bureaucratic system, which has done little else than bring discussion of what ought to be done. This process has been recurring, and as a result, progress has halted often on some such basis as insufficient funds. Health of the Bay, a subcommittee of the San Diego Bay Advisory Committee for Ecological Assessment, was formed to discuss Bill 68 with members of San Diego Bay clubs. The bill proposes to clean up San Diego Bay by beseeching superior California courts for funds. Every month they gather to discuss new developments and strategies according to their members' qualifications and abilities. Members include the San Diego Sierra Club, US Navy, SD Port, the Scripps Institute of Oceanography (SIO) and local fisheries. Their primary concern is networking

with the right people to get the various tasks accomplished, which make up the assessment donated or at least to stay within their budget. Because of money shortages their ecological assessments are rather limited. Senate Bill 68, which is now in the process of being drafted, outlines subjects that compose the framework for future challenges and opportunities in caring for San Diego Bay.

The six criteria included in the report are physical features, biology, habitat, water quality, sediment quality, toxicology, sources, and historical context. In a legislative context Senate Bill 68 is an evaluation of historic data and trends in the overall health of San Diego Bay, including, but not limited to, trends in pollutant levels and trends in the numbers and diversity of species. The identification of habitat enhancement projects in the Integrated Natural Resources Management Plan for San Diego Bay that may be necessary to provide increased population and diversity for species within San Diego Bay are listed.

As an example of the group's collaboration, there is MEC-Weston. MEC-Weston, the lead consultant, has finished mapping the five strata, including freshwater inputs, shallow water, deep water, marinas, and port/industrial. The depths for the shallow and deep water are consistent with those in the Integrated Natural Resources Management Plan for San Diego Bay (INRMP). Their field work has identified the following monitoring indicators: sediment (chemistry, benthic community, and toxicity), fish (tissue), and water quality (chemistry, toxicity, and general parameters). MEC-Weston has also compiled data on San Diego Bay from approximately 20 sources, from which they will write an annotated bibliography. Data sources include SCCWRP Bight work and TMDL data from RWQCB, among others. Some data is proprietary and not available. A sentiment was expressed from the Subcommittee that we should continue to ask for this data. It was also suggested that we should look for sources of bird data. The Natural History Museum has just released the San Diego County Bird Atlas.

How is this applicable to the field guide? A public endeavor to preserve San Diego Bay for the public's enjoyment and as a place rich in a recreational sense and critical for the inhabitants of the distinct communities is necessary. By assessing the health of the Bay, proper measures can be taken to secure that these things are salvaged for its inhabitants and users.

The first draft of Bill 68 will be out during July; the members will then be able to review it, and make any changes as they see fit. Finally, at the end of the year the final copy will be drafted and a case will be made to the Sacramento legislation to see where the plans head.

Perspectives Off the Bay

Herein lies the truth behind the field guide known as Perspectives on the Bay, *not the marketing information, not the scientific data, or any other attempt to mislead the reader through some "objective" portrayal of reality. Instead, herein one will find an honest journal, perhaps amusing, perhaps comical, perhaps a wee bit cynical, yet always truly honest. Here begins a behind-the-scenes look at our work: a student's perspective in the guise of an innocent travel log.*

Boat Channel Bridge – Proud Peacocks

The Boat Channel Bridge, eu-phemistically labeled the Spanish Landing, is comprised of a mass of rocky hills, muddy flats, a small grass strip with just a few trees that make shade a premium, reserved only for the elite, or at least the fleet of foot. Walking distance from our school, the location was an easily reached introduction to the Field Guide Project (FGP).

Perhaps the presence of the media there that day made it the more important. Ever present at our school, a camera crew showed itself this first day of our FGP. There they were, waiting for us, a news crew which desired nothing more than to hear about our ambitions and take video of our labors. There we were, working down below, the first day of transects, strutting proudly like peacocks, wishing, of course, to look our best for the cameras and the possible fame to ensue.

Point Loma Seafood – Scavenging Seagulls

The seagulls claim their prey and it turned out to be our lunch. In the second trip we undertook for the FGP, food became the center of our discourse. Point Loma Seafood is a tasty treat, one in which lunch is an enjoyable activity. Yet as we were to discover, even here we see the effects of pollution, paper cups. Flotsam and jetsam float at our feet.

While eating lunch in the outdoor courtyard, one must watch his food carefully. Turn your back for a minute and your sandwich shall no longer be your lunch, but that of a hungry bird, the seagulls especially. Perhaps worse are the small brothers-in-arms to the seagulls, the unholy alliance of pigeons and sparrows. This batch not only will steal your lunch while your back is turned, but may swarm the isolated diner. Their hunger drives them not to care for the wayward eater's happiness, peace of mind, or lost chow.

All and all, it is surprising that there is this much life in this place. Life which can, at times even take surprising forms. In this place where, later in the day, as we began yet again to do our transect work, we are approached by a man in a full biohazard suit! Breathing air, and watching us with a knowing gaze as we traverse and transect down amongst the muck. Does he think we might be trying to grow a third arm?

Boat Channel – Bolting Bunnies

On the third trip for the FGP, we become aware that the marching to and fro will not abate. It has caused some complaints, but our leaders still walk quickly onwards, as if some great vision or excitement lay just ahead. Perhaps, had we thought about it, a touch of worry should have come across us, to be led by such madmen.

For the first time in the FGP, we are going to the very place that bears the name the Boat Channel. The source of last year's student study, the place whose precious and previous Field Guide has been held up for our perpetual adoration, the very namesake of the study of the Bay. It is interesting perhaps

that our third encounter is in reality so close to our school. We walk along the Rosecrans Street, worried about how far we have to go, yet looking ahead we see our teachers have disappeared. Quickly a head reappears out of a small hole in the fencing. A sign warns in large block letters: No Trespassing. "Come along." The teacher merrily shouts.

Yet do we obey the sign? Not a chance. Instead we venture onwards and inwards, initially hidden by high hedges, blocking those who may spot us, just as they remain hidden to us. Like rabbits, we reach the edge of the shelter. Between us and the safety of the Boat Channel, we face and must cross a vast and barren expanse - the McMillan Construction Zone! With that we began to venture, tentatively at first, yet gaining speed with our boost in confidence. Near the end, however, we are spotted; a large, yellow, mammoth caterpillar machine, a dump truck and other assorted construction equipment barrel quickly towards us. With haste we run, jumping, even hopping, for the hurdle at the Gates of the Boat Channel. To our dismay, the equipment simply continues on about their work, not caring or noticing our existence. We head down the serene path towards the Boat Channel, ready to begin yet another day of transects.

Hornblower / Midway – Heaven to Hell

Down by the docks at the ragged foot of downtown San Diego sits a boat which might blow its own horn. The "Hornblower" is at its port of call – the ebb and flow of passengers coming and going show just how busy this place can be. Will all this hustle-bustle cause our luxury liner to blow her horn again?

As we arrive we are immediately dismissed for lunch and instructed to be back in an hour. Our transportation has gotten us there early; what a better thing to do but eat? Sitting, eating fresh seafood, birds watch with a jealous gaze. (Might they have earned their stripes at Point Loma Seafood?)

Who should come out of the Hornblower but a cohort of students. A field trip from some elementary school. Sitting and observing this phenomenon was interesting, for first one, then two, then a group of five or six would come down off the gangplank, disembarking from the boat. Soon a sea of them flooded the sidewalk, all of them housed in their own blue shirts, broken only by the occasional pillar of a parent, to which the small ones cling as if their very lives depended on it.

With that it is our turn, to board the very same boat, and go out, with our own tide. We spend time upon the blue sparkling Bay, fresh air awakens even the drowsiest amongst us. After a turn around the Bay, on the way homeward we move towards a military carrier, observing its vast and ominous nature, a desolate concrete jungle, a ship with its own area code. While appearing to be a skeleton of hulking bleakness, once aboard it becomes a ship that still manages to be cramped. How could something so miserable employ so many people? How, while in that prison, could the occupants not revolt? We, who had just gone from the blissful freedom of the Hornblower to the pinched prison of the Midway, were highly qualified to judge.

Boat Channel – Bird Ball

Ahh, the novelty has worn off our work; we might even call it boring now. To be stuck yet again at the Boat Channel, to be there for hours on end. We are all eager to finish the transect; to finish that massive quantity of work so that we might pursue more pleasurable activities. It is sad to say, but we rush through our transects, hurrying to count all the little creatures and critters. Then we dash up the slimy slopes, trying not to appear too eager, even though we wish nothing more than to be free of the mush-filled and marsh-covered pit.

The pit is to be feared. There lies the torture and agony that go with

drudging about, the fear of never knowing where or when one is to sink to the waist, or when one will experience again the temporary joy of being on firm ground. Once up away from the sloshy shore, groups of boys begin to play football, in love anew with the simple freedom of throwing the ball long and far. A freedom we envy, that ball enjoys the kind of flight that just before only birds could obtain. We track the ball, watch it gently spiral its way downwards, ready to make contact with another thrower's waiting arms, sent again into its glorious flight.

SPLASH! It is all over. There is no more football, there is nothing, the game is gone. A pollution-filled channel fills our senses. And there, halfway across it bobs the symbol of our joy, a single football, waiting there. A desperate cry goes out, a call to rescue our drowning companion. We call for the return of our once free ball, to return it to its previous flight.

SPLASH! Our brother goes into the drink, willing to sacrifice for the good of the collective. He will save our leather-covered companion. Cradling the ball gingerly on its journey back to shore, he is greeted upon emergence by the shocked stares of his comrades-in-arms. Is this a drowned rat, returning with some morsel of soggy, browncheese or our savior?

Scripps – Dollhouse Doo Doo

The Scripps research facility houses some very impressive bits of technology. Boats full of gear, ready to go out to sea, to make their way across the world. They do what we have been doing with our daily transects, yet on a far more grand and global scale.

However, despite their grandiosity of mission, one cannot help but compare those researchers aboard their vessels to ants, even children. They swarm across the boats, amongst the many maze-like bunches of cables or buoys or stacks of food. Amongst the seemingly endless piles, they seem to transform their boat into nothing more than a floating wardrobe into which

one very large child has stuffed all his or her toys, clothes and other gear. Playful scientists make ready their floating dollhouse laboratories.

A mere minute's walk from this hub of research-readying activity there is a tranquil beach, the first of its kind that we've seen with signs of habitation. There is surely less pollution here, we surmise. It will be a safe place, we think. So idle chatter enters our minds; we sit and stew with our groups in our own carefree manner. We have no desire to get what we now perceive as drudgery started, yet we still manage to present an eager face when some excited teacher gives rise to a question.

As we walk across the sand, the tide ebbs in and out, lapping gently at our feet. It is almost peaceful here; the air itself carries a sweet softness. "THERE IS POO IN THE WATER!" someone shouts.

A small brown creature with yellow spots, bearing a striking resemblance to feces is bobbing in and out with the tide. When this creature became stuck, lodged in fact further up the bank, and unable to return to its watery home, we got our opportunity to take a closer look. It is not a "poo" but rather a "navanax," a remarkably odd sea slug. With a blue rim and yellow stripes, it has a pretty appearance, despite the names we've called it. This bit of excitement over, we say our farewells to the poo-navanax, and each go our separate ways. Back to our familiar transects with their more common and comforting assortments of barnacles.

Boat Channel Mapping – Sand Skippers

There is a competition in Japan. A long path is made of reeds, not thick enough to support the weight of a single person for a prolonged period of time. This path of reeds is extended off the side of a boat. Then the smallest, lightest and fastest, sprint. They run down the path, grab a baton and run back to the boat. A one-man relay against time and the crashing force of reeds sinking into the water. Speed is essential; without it, one will take the plunge, not knowing from where the next breath of air shall come, or worse still, lose the competition.

With that in mind, let us return to the Boat Channel, and our antics within it. This, our last visit, is unique: We are not to complete transects (what glorious relief!) but rather to attempt to make a map. Pencil, paper, rulers and our imagination take over. Some sit and scribble, while others, the more serious amongst us, decide to count our paces down the length and distance of things. To do so, we take our place along the very cusp of the water line, and from one end

of the channel to the next we must go.

We have found our own version of the Japanese reed race. Sand, like reeds on water, cannot support one's weight. Instead one is left with a single goal, to sprint as fast as possible across said sands, not letting them engulf one's foot, leg, or body, but rather to laugh triumphantly as the maw bites at empty air, seconds too late, the foot already gone. The measurements taken, we sit, beyond the dark and sandy reach, leaving naught behind but footsteps atop the sand. We are triumphant.

Coronado Island – First-Person Fear

While we visited the beloved Island during the day, the place is better visited late at night. There is a mysterious air about the place then, it is dark, cold and damp, far different from that sunny place so often depicted on those tourist postcards. Now it is night and dark. I've come back to sit triumphantly above the shore of the day's transect study. I view downtown's lights, presenting their spectacular display just across the Bay. Such beauty.

A cold dank fog rolls over the water. Not so much seen as felt. A dark chill absorbs me. In the blink of an eye the stadium disappears. The fog rolls farther inwards. Another blink and all of Downtown has disappeared beneath the dark, impenetrable and evil hand.

Perhaps the mysterious air has gotten too mysterious. I wonder what all the other people are doing? I wonder what treachery is afoot under tonight's veil of darkness. The restaurants, food, pleasant neighborhoods, busy buildings are now only a memory. Dark undertones take their place, dark depths hide all seemingly good things. It is weather like this when dark and criminal things happen. Why am I here so late at night on this secluded Island? Those daylit transect studies were happier times. I run. I'm done for. This travel log is over!

by Zeke Koziol

FOOD WEB

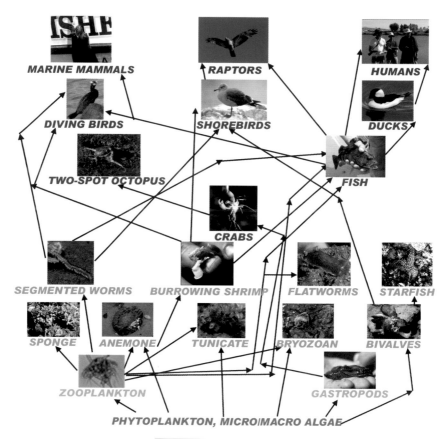

MARINE MAMMALS

RAPTORS

HUMANS

DIVING BIRDS

SHOREBIRDS

DUCKS

TWO-SPOT OCTOPUS

FISH

CRABS

SEGMENTED WORMS   BURROWING SHRIMP   FLATWORMS   STARFISH

SPONGE   ANEMONE   TUNICATE   BRYOZOAN   BIVALVES

ZOOPLANKTON   GASTROPODS

PHYTOPLANKTON, MICRO/MACRO ALGAE

COLOR KEY

RED: QUATERNARY

PURPLE: TERTIARY

BLUE: SECONDARY

YELLOW: PRIMARY

GREEN: PRODUCERS

In order for most animals to survive, other animals must be consumed. This fact of nature creates a hierarchy of the powerful and the eaten. More commonly known as the food chain or food web, the tango between predator and prey is a complex and essential part of any habitat. The intertidal zone is no exception to the chain of command that dictates who eats who.

At the very bottom of this chain are the microscopic organisms called plankton. Since phytoplankton (microscopic plants) generate their own energy from the sun, they do not need to consume other organisms; hence they are not predators of any kind, only prey. Other types of zooplankton (microscopic animals), sponges, tunicates, barnacles, and tube snails all feed on the phytoplankton as their primary source of energy.

These animals are prey themselves. The next level up on the food chain brings more complex and predatory animals such as crabs, octopi, fish, and some birds. These creatures will consume the lowest order of predators in order to gain nutrients. Even this tier is not safe from predators in the intertidal zone. Large birds of prey, diving birds, and large fish will consume the middle tier of predators. In order to catch prey efficiently, this class of animal has evolved with more predatory features such as speed, stealth, and cunning.

At the top of the natural food chain inside San Diego Bay are the dolphins, seals, and sea lions. These marine mammals hunt their prey with deadly efficiency and have no natural predators in the immediate habitat. The lack of predators makes these creatures the top of the natural food chain.

While dolphins may not have any natural predators, the ultimate killer, man, is always a major threat to the entire food chain. In order for animals to survive, their prey and every tier underneath their prey must survive. If the phytoplankton would die off for some reason, then the shrimp would die because they would not have anything to eat. The fish would die because there are no shrimp to eat, and the birds and dolphins would die because there are no fish to eat. This chain reaction is one of the reasons why food webs are extremely important to any ecosystem, especially one as affected by human development as the San Diego Bay is.

Losing the most primitive forms of food in a food web is not the only thing that could cause an ecological collapse. If a major predator should become extinct or rare, then its prey develops and multiplies unchecked. If there are no predators to eat the prey, then it is possible for the prey to multiply to a point where they collapse the ecosystem from overpopulations.

Glossary

Asexual reproduction: Reproduction without eggs and sperm (e.g. bacteria are asexual as they multiply by dividing).

Biarticulate: Consisting of two articles or segments.

Bivalve: A mollusk whose body is enclosed by a pair of hard shells.

Calcareous: Contains calcium carbonate.

Carnivore: An animal that eats other animals.

Carotenoid: Any of a group of red, orange, and yellow accessory pigments (coloring matter) of plants or algae.

Caudal: Pertaining to the tail.

Chelipeds: Whole appendage bearing chela (claw or pincer).

Cilia: Hair-like organelles extending from the membrane of many eukaryotic (containing a nucleus and other membrane-bound organelles) cells; often function in locomotion.

Cirri: Small, flexible appendages present on some invertebrates, including barnacles and annelids.

Coalesce: To fuse, blend, merge, unite, or cause to grow together.

Copepods: Any of a large subclass (Copepoda) of usually minute freshwater and marine crustaceans that form an important element of the plankton in the marine environment and in some fresh waters.

Cortex: The outer layer of the cerebrum (brain), densely packed with nerve cells.

Detritus: Particles from decaying plants and animals.

Diatom: Unicellular algae capable of photosynthesis and characterized by producing a thin outer shell made of silica (glass).

Dioecious: Having the organs of the sexes upon distinct individuals.

Discordant: A twin pair (or set of individuals) in which one member exhibits a certain trait and the other does not; belonging to divergent species.

Distal: Farthest from the body.

Dorsal: Refers to the back of an organism, as in the dorsal fin of a shark.

Echolocation: The process by which an animal locates itself with respect to other animals and objects by emitting sound waves and sensing the pattern of the reflected sound waves.

Elongated: Made or grown longer; having notably more length than width; being long and slender.

Esophagus: Portion of the gut between the mouth and stomach in the anterior neck.

Exoskeleton: An external skeleton or supportive covering of an animal, as for example, the shell coverings of a crustacean, the calcium carbonate secretions of stony corals, or the bony plates of an armadillo.

Flagella: Long hair-like organelles at the surface of the cell with capacity for movement.

Foliose: Leaf-like; bearing leaves.

Follicle: A small anatomical sac, cavity, or deep narrow-mouthed depression (e.g. a hair follicle).

Gamete: Mature male or female reproductive cell (sperm or ovum) with a haploid set of chromosomes.

Gestation: The process, also known as pregnancy, by which a mammalian female carries a live offspring from conception until it develops to the point (birth) where the offspring is capable of living outside the womb.

Girdle (chiton): The outer rim or leathery border of chitons.

Gonads: Primary sex organs; ovaries in the female and testes in the male.

Gregarious: Tending to form a group with others of the same kind.

Haploid: A single set of chromosomes (half the full set of genetic material), present in the egg and sperm cells of animals and in the egg and pollen cells of plants.

Herbivore: A plant-eating animal.

Hermaphrodite: An animal or plant having both male and female reproductive organs.

Intertidal: The zone between high and low tide.

Isopod: Any of a large order of sessile-eyed crustaceans with the body composed of seven free thoracic segments, each bearing a similar pair of legs.

Larvae: The young and immature form of an animal, which must change to become an adult.

Locomotion: The ability or power to move.

Mantle: A protective layer of epidermis in mollusks or brachiopods that secretes a substance forming the shell.

Membrane: A pliable sheet of tissue that covers or lines or connects organs or cells of animals.

Monogamous: The condition in which a single male and female form a prolonged and more or less exclusive breeding relationship.

Monomorphic: An organism whose sex cannot be determined by just looking at them.

Mottled: Any material that contains spots of different colors or shades.

Mysids: Group of small, shrimp-like crustaceans characterized by possessing a ventral brood pouch.

Neuron: The main actors in the brain, neurons are cells that issue and receive electrical signals to and from other parts of the body.

Nymph: A larva of an insect with incomplete metamorphosis.

Organelle: A subcellular structure having a specialized function, for example, the mitochondrion, the chloroplast, or the spindle apparatus.

Ostracods: Small mobile marine with right and left valves for shells and an indistinctly segmented body.

Ovaries: Female sex organs.

Palp: A lateral appendage of the lower jaw or the maxilliped (a paired appendage on the posterior and ventral edge of the cephalon (the head, or anteriormost body unit)).

Papillose: Covered with fleshy, nipple-like projections on an animal's mantle.

Paragnath: One of the two lobes which form the metastome (lower lip) of Crustacea; one of the small, horny, toothlike jaws of certain annelids.

Pectoral: Of, pertaining to, situated, or occurring in or on the chest.

Peristomium: The first segment of the earthworm's body; contains the mouth.

Phytoplankton: Minute free-floating aquatic plants.

Planktonic: Free-floating; drifting, rather than swimming.

Plumage: The feathers of a bird.

Polychaetes: A class of marine worms and their free-swimming larvae.

Polymorphic: A species having many different forms.

Proboscis: An elongated appendage of a living organism. The most common usage is to refer to the tubular feeding and sucking organ of certain invertebrates like insects, worms and mollusks.

Prostomium: The lobe of skin that projects out in front of the peristomium (first body segment). It is located above the mouth, and there are three different formations.

Radula: A flexible tongue-like organ in some molluscs that consists of rows of horny teeth on the surface.

Raucous: Unpleasantly loud and harsh.

Regurgitate: To bring undigested or partially digested food up from the stomach to the mouth, as some birds and animals do to feed their young.

Reticulation: A pattern formed by obliquely (slanting or sidelong direction or position) intersecting threads or linear ridges of ornament (surface sculpture standing out in relief on shell surface).

Scavenger: An animal that eats the dead remains and wastes of other animals and plants.

Sculpin: An ugly little fish found in trout streams that trout love to eat.

Sessile: Organisms that remain attached to a substrate.

Substrate: The material making up the base upon which an organism lives or to which it is attached.

Subtidal: Below the level of the lowest tide.

Syrinx: The "voice box" in the throat near where the bronchial tubes and the trachea join. In song birds, the syrinx is the organ that makes singing possible.

Terga: The back, or back plates of an animal.

Transverse: Lying or being across, or in a crosswise direction.

Tremolo: The quick repetition of a note; the alternation between two notes as rapidly as possible.

Trochophore: A small, free-swimming, larval stage of some aquatic invertebrates such as mussels and clams; trochophores swim using cilia, rather than flagella or some other method.

Unicellular: Single-celled.

Valve: One of the two halves of the shell of a bivalve mollusk.

Vertebrae: The bones of the spinal column.

References

Abbott, Patrick L. The Rise and Fall of San Diego. San Diego: Sunbelt Publications, 1999.

Barnes, Robert D. Invertebrate Zoology. Philadelphia, PA: Saunders College. 1980.

Behrens, David W. Pacific Coast Nudibranchs. Los Osos: Sea Challengers, 1980.

Brandon, Jeffrey L. and Rokop, Frank J. Life Between the Tides. San Diego, CA: American Southwest Publishing Company of San Diego. 1985.

Davis, Chuck. California Reefs. San Francisco: Chronicle Books,1991.

Eschmeyer, William N., Earl S. Herald and Howard Hammann. Pacific Coast Fishes. New York: Houghton Mifflin Company. 1983

Gotshall, D. and L. Laurent. Pacific Coast Subtidal Marine Invertebrates. Monterey, CA: Sea Challengers, 1980.

Gotshall, Daniel W. Pacific Coast Inshore Fishes. Los Osos, CA: Sea Challengers. 1981.

Gotshall, Daniel W., and Laurence L. Laurent. Pacific Coast Subtidal Marine Invertebrates: A Fishwatchers' Guide. Monterey: Sea Challengers, 1979.

Harris, Leon C. Concepts in Zoology. New York: HarperCollins Publishers Inc. 1992.

Hedgpeth, Joel , and Sam Hinton. Common Seashore Life of Southern California. Happy Camp: Naturegraph, 1961.

Ingmanson, Dale E. and William J, Wallace. Oceanography: An Introduction. Belmont, CA: Wadsworth Publishing Company. 1973.

Knopf, Alfred A. The Audubon Society Field Guide to North American Fishes, Whales & Dolphines. Part 1st ed. New York: 1977

Morris, Percy A. A Field Guide to Pacific Coast Shells. 2nd ed. Boston: Houghton Mifflin Company, 1966.

Morris, R. H., D. P. Abbot, and E. C. Haderlie. Intertidal Invertebrates of California. Stanford, CA: Stanford University Press. 1980.

225

Peterson, Roger T. Western Birds. New York, Houghton Mifflin Company. 1990.

Rickets, Ed, and John Steinbeck. The Other Shores. Part 1st ed. Eureka, California: Mad River P, 1978.

Ricketts, Edward F. and Jack Calvin. Between Pacific Tides. 4th Ed. Revised by J.W. Hedgpath. Stanford University Press. 1968.

Sept, J. D. The Beachcomber's Guide to Seashore Life of California. Maderia Park: Harbour, 2002.

Smith, Deboyd L. A Guide to Marine Coastal Plankton and Marine Invertebrate Larvae. Debuque, IA: Kendall/Hunt Publishing Company. 1977.

Sumich, James L. An Introduction to the Biology of Marine Life. Dubuque: Wm. C. Brown, 1996.

Sumich, James L. Biology of Marine Life. Dubuque, IA: Wm. C. Brown Publishers. 1976.

Udvary, Miklos D. National Audubon Society Field Guide to North American Birds. New York. Chantcleer Press. 1994.

Unitt, Philip. San Diego County Bird Atlas. San Diego, CA. Ibis Publishing Company. 2004.

Vanner, Michael. The Encyclopedia of North American Birds. New York: Barnes & Nobles Books, 2003.

This book is brought to you by "The Editors"